D1572104

No. 242 Squadron
The Canadian Years

No. 242 Squadron
The Canadian Years

The story of the RAF's 'all-Canadian' Fighter Squadron

Hugh Halliday

Canadian Cataloguing in Publication Data

Halliday, Hugh A., 1940-
    No. 242 Squadron, the Canadian years

Includes index.
Bibliography: p.
ISBN 0-920002-09-9

1. Great Britain. Royal Air Force. 242 Squadron—
History. 2. World War, 1939-1945—Aerial operations,
British. 3. World War, 1939-1945—Aerial operations,
Canadian. I. Title.

D786.H34   940.54'4941   C81-090087-4

*First published in 1981 by Canada's Wings, Inc.,
Box 393, Stittsville, Ontario K0A 3G0, Canada.*

*Cover art by Rikki Karellen Cameron
Printed by The Intelligencer, Belleville, Ontario*

CONTENTS

Introduction

Why a history of No. 242 Squadron? The simple answer is that no proper account of that unit has ever been published before. Even this work, covering as it does only the "Canadian" period of the squadron, cannot be considered a complete study. In the interests of telling a consistent story, however, this writer has concentrated upon the period ending September 1941, when the posting from the squadron of Flight Lieutenant R.D. Grassick severed the link between the original "Canadian" unit as formed in 1939, and the cosmopolitan squadron that No. 242 had become. The tale of its further existence is left to other authors.

No. 242 (Canadian) Squadron holds particular interest to students of Canadian military history. Its origins were highly political, arising out of this country's desire to be represented in the fighting line by a distinctly Canadian formation at the earliest possible moment. This could best be done by using Canadians who were already overseas and could be grouped into a small but identifiable national unit. Only the Royal Air Force, with its small battle organizations (squadrons) and large numbers of Canadians enrolled, was able to provide an opportunity for such a semi-official national presence.

1

The genesis of No. 242 lay in Anglo-Canadian talks to organize the British Commonwealth Air Training Plan. During the course of these discussions Canadian officials insisted as a condition of co-operation that uniquely Canadian, RCAF squadrons be formed overseas, and provision for such units was made in Article 15 of the resultant agreement. No. 242 was a stop-gap measure, decided upon even before the BCATP negotiations had been concluded. It was assumed that eventually it would become an RCAF unit. These plans fell apart in the spring of 1940, partly because the RCAF itself lost interest, partly because it proved to be impractical to maintain its Canadian composition during the Battle of France. Nevertheless, the squadron continued to be manned by a significant proportion of Canadians, and to attract public attention on that account, until the spring of 1941.

To say that no detailed history of No. 242 has ever been *published* is not to say that nothing has been *written* about that unit. A glance at the footnotes and bibliography will show that many publications have referred to the squadron to greater or lesser degrees. There have also been some manuscripts developed that did not enjoy general circulation.

For this author the most important source was a narrative entitled *The All Canadian Squadron*, compiled in 1941 by the late Wing Commander F.H. Hitchins. The document was based upon the Operational Record Book (Forms 540 and 541) of No. 242 Squadron, complemented by references to Combat Reports filed by various members of the squadron. Where No. 242's records were vague or missing, Wing Commander Hitchins (a meticulous researcher who has left a generation of aviation historians in his debt) went to related sources, such as the Operational Record Books of units fighting alongside No. 242. Hitchins does not appear often in the footnotes of this narrative; his role is understated because the basic account was his from the beginning. This introduction may be interpreted as an extended footnote acknowledging his seminal role.[1]

Another source of information was a card file compiled by Wing Commander Hitchins on Canadians who had enrolled directly in the RAF before the outbreak of hostilities and early in the war

1. Copies of *The All Canadian Squadron* are held by the Canadian Armed Forces Directorate of History, by the University of Western Ontario (Hitchins Papers), and by this writer.

itself—the CAN/RAF personnel. Insofar as No. 242's members were concerned, the cards largely duplicated the information already found in *The All Canadian Squadron*. They did throw much light, however, on the backgrounds of squadron personnel and on the later activities of those who survived their experiences with No. 242; they also proved informative about other CAN/RAF people whose careers, though not bound up directly with that unit, were in one way or another instructive in placing No. 242 in the context of RAF policies and operations. A series of squadron narratives prepared by Hitchins on other RAF units in the 1939-41 period were also helpful in viewing the overall environment in which No. 242 functioned.[2]

Beyond the basic Hitchins material (complemented by this writer's own consultation of the squadron's Operational Record Book in February 1980), a considerable body of information was unearthed from other sources. Some of this data was primary information, gleaned from documents of the period; more was obtained from secondary sources—books and magazine articles dating from the wartime period through to the present. Many people also gave of their time to provide recollections of their experiences in No. 242.

Not all sources are equally reliable or accurate. The narrative that follows may not coincide exactly with the memories of men who served with the squadron—memories filtered and sometimes unconsciously altered in the passage of forty years. Nor are all secondary or primary documents of equal value. In compiling this history, the author has had to weigh statements from various sources against one another. Sometimes such sources have contradicted each other on points of fact. In the process of weeding out errors, or at least pointing out anomalies, the writer has established what might be described as a hierarchy of historical credibility.

For much of the period under review the Operational Record Book of No. 242 Squadron was the most important document—a daily accounting of events compiled under official auspices. No. 242's ORB presented some problems in that it has a total gap for the period of June 1st to 13th, 1940, and many entries are vague, particularly those covering June 14th to 30th, 1940. Since that month was particularly crucial to the unit's development, this

2. Copies of these are held by the Directorate of History, Ottawa, and by the author.

situation was particularly trying. On a few occasions, too, No. 242's "official" account of events was clearly at variance with several other sources; a notable example is the ORB's statement of May 24th, 1940 that Pilot Officers Hill and Mitchell had been shot down by flak, when other evidence pointed strongly to a mid-air collision.

Beyond the ORB were several other official documents of only slightly less weight. Correspondence between Canadian and British officials clearly spelled out the policies leading to No. 242's creation. Combat Reports were important contemporary accounts of aerial battles, drawn up by the pilots themselves with their unit Intelligence Officers minutes after landing. Pilots' logbooks yielded much information; these, too, are documents describing immediate events, although it was found that in May and June 1940 those kept by N.K. Stansfeld and R.D. Grassick did not always conform to other records.

Contemporary reports by personnel were also used—personal diaries, statements to reporters, and letters home that were reprinted in Canadian newspapers. They may not always have been objective or fully accurate, but they were observations recorded close to the very events described, distorted only by the confusion of the times. Newspaper reports were also contemporary, but the writers were removed from the events, and erred frequently. The author's task was to sort out wheat from chaff.

Published works were more or less valuable according to the sources upon which they were based. Histories such as F.K. Mason's *Battle Over Britain* and L.F. Ellis' *The War in France and Flanders, 1939-40* were particularly useful in giving the overall situations during the Battles of France and Britain, and for describing what was happening on the German side. Bernard Dupérier's *La Veille Equipe* was virtually the diary of that officer, published with a few additional comments on his part, and thus ranked with other diary material in accuracy. Some books had to be treated cautiously, either because they included generous helpings of wartime propaganda (*Come the Three Corners*, by Sir Harry Brittain), or they showed signs of careless research (*Reach for the Sky* by Paul Brickhill, a great source of anecdotes about No. 242, but erring on small points, for example the mythology surrounding Richard Cork's "DFC").

Personal recollections, whether oral or written in 1980, were the most difficult of all sources to weigh. The events described occurred some 40 years in the past, and were very important to the people concerned; they would not easily forget their adventures. Nevertheless, time does warp some memories more than others. If an interviewee's recollections were contradicted by documents from 1940-41, then the documents obviously carried greater weight. Consistency between recollections and documents (when comparison was possible) suggested accurate memories of items not otherwise recorded. Furthermore, a person's retention of some documents from No. 242's days—logbooks, diaries, scrapbooks—would clearly serve to keep his memories in order. Thus, the accounts given by James Howitt, Noel Stansfeld, and Ian Arthur were especially valuable; their records jogged some memories and kept the sequence of events in order.

Many people have contributed to the compilation of this account; most will be mentioned either in the text, footnotes, or picture credits. Yet a few additional acknowledgements are in order. The staff of the Photographic Division, Imperial War Museum, reacted quickly to my inquiries about pictorial material. Similarly, the personnel of the RAF Museum at Hendon were models of co-operation, responding promptly, thoroughly, and with much initiative; Mr. A.E. Cormack of that organization located and copied valuable documents describing No. 242's contribution to the Battle of France and to 1941 operations. The RAF Records Centre was helpful in supplying service details of some obscure members. Here in Canada, the Canadian Armed Forces Directorate of History aided with material on the few RCAF personnel who served in No. 242; Win McIntosh and Philip Chaplin were in the forefront of the Directorate's assistance. Finally, Mr. Ludwig Kosche proved to be a good friend and severe editor, reading the manuscript through three drafts and suggesting numerous improvements.

Some personalities stand out strongly in this account; others receive little more attention than the mention of their names. Readers should remember that fame or recognition does not necessarily imply special merit. Many a fine pilot has endured the same hardships and perils as his more illustrious companions, served honourably, and died without laurels. Moreover, we should recognize that many of No. 242's personnel are utterly anonymous in any narrative. Particular tribute is owing to those who kept things running—the mechanics, armourers, signals personnel, and administrative staff. No. 242, like any operational unit, was a spear; the pilots were the sharp fighting tip, but the driving shaft behind them was the army of "erks", "spies", and "grocers" who laboured on, knowing they were vital but obscure. To all staff, aircrew and groundcrew alike, this work is dedicated; it is, after all, their story.

The End and the Beginning

On May 6th, 1942, Air Vice Marshal Harold Edwards, the Air Officer in Chief of RCAF Overseas Headquarters in London, England, despatched a letter to the Director of Organization, Air Ministry. His subject was No. 242 (Canadian) Squadron, a Royal Air Force formation which had been originally organized as a unit of Canadians serving in the RAF. Now, however, he was requesting that the "Canadian" designation be dropped from the unit's nomenclature. His reasoning was simply and directly stated:

> This squadron has long ceased to have any truly Canadian representation or connection, and in view of the number of Canadian squadrons now in operation with the R.A.F. it seems illogical to continue to denote this squadron as "Canadian". [1]

Edwards repeated his request in another letter three days later. On this occasion he added a comment on the initial concept that had given birth to No. 242 Squadron:

1. Air Vice Marshal H. Edwards to Director of Organization, Air Ministry, May 6th, 1942. RCAF Overseas Headquarters File S.1-5, Policy—No. 242 (Canadian) Squadron, RAF. Held by Canadian Armed Forces Directorate of History (hereafter referred to as DHist), reference 181.009 D.3564.

It was a splendid arrangement in the early stages and its inception is very much appreciated, but it is considered that there is now a possibility of confusion.[2]

The request was granted; on May 21st, 1942, the Air Ministry informed Canadian authorities that No. 242 was losing its "Canadian" appellation.[3] Indeed the unit was even then being reborn. Having ceased in fact to be a "Canadian" unit by April 1941, it had gone on to intensive service in the Far East. In March 1942, caught up in desperate fighting in Sumatra and Java, No. 242 had virtually disintegrated. At the time of Edwards' correspondence with Air Ministry it was being reformed as a *Spitfire* squadron in England, with no attempt being made to cast it again in a Canadian image.

* * * * *

The formation of No. 242 (Canadian) Squadron had been an idea born in the midst of negotiations between British and Canadian authorities over the formation of the British Commonwealth Air Training Plan (BCATP) and the nature of Canadian participation in the war. It represented a half-way point between the integration of Royal Canadian Air Force personnel into British squadrons and the formation of all-Canadian units under exclusive RCAF control, a goal nominally achieved by the Canadian government through Article 15 of the BCATP agreements.

When the war began there were more than 1,000 Canadian members of the RAF either serving as aircrew in RAF formations or undergoing aircrew training. These were the so-called "CAN/RAF" personnel—Canadians who had by-passed the RCAF in favour of direct enlistment in the RAF. Some had been around since the First World War and now held senior rank; others had joined in the 1920's and presently held Squadron Leader and Wing Commander rank. The great majority had arrived in growing numbers from 1935 onwards, sometimes with partial RAF sponsorship but most often on their own initiative. The tiny RCAF with its limited personnel requirements seemed to offer little opportunity for adventure and advancement. Together with numerous Canadians who had enrolled as groundcrew in the RAF, there was clearly enough manpower

2. Edwards to Air Vice Marshal L.H. Hollinghurst, May 9th, 1942. *Ibid*.

3. Air Ministry to Edwards, May 21st, 1942. *Ibid*.

available to form a squadron composed largely (though not entirely) of Canadians.

No sooner had Canada declared war upon Germany on September 10th, 1939, than the manner in which this country would participate came under discussion between the British High Commissioner to Canada, Sir Gerald Campbell, and Canadian authorities, most notably Prime Minister Mackenzie King.

On September 13th Sir Gerald despatched a telegram to his superiors at the Dominions Office, London.[4] It touched upon several points, including Canada's willingness to have "Canadian Air Force units as soon as sufficient trained personnel are available overseas for this purpose". These units, however, would have to be equipped in the United Kingdom, Canada having virtually no modern service aircraft at that time.[5]

The British were happy at the prospect of having Dominion squadrons added to the RAF's strength. Not only would they augment the Royal Air Force, but they would also serve, it was hoped, to impress the Germans, the British public, and Britain's allies with the solidarity of the Empire/Commonwealth. On September 26th a message was sent to Sir Gerald, advising him of a suggestion that was being put before Australia, Canada, and New Zealand:

> Air Council would welcome, as an immediate step, formation of a Royal Canadian Air Force squadron overseas at the earliest possible date. . . . Such a squadron might be provided from trained Canadian personnel whether already in this country or despatched specially, service aircraft being provided here. Total personnel should, if possible, be sufficient, not only to fill squadron establishment, but also to replace initial wastage.[6]

4. The peculiar nature of British Imperial ties was most evident in the numerous departments dealing with components of the whole—the India Office for India, Colonial Office for colonies such as Kenya or Malta, and the Dominions Office for the self-governing dominions (Australia, Canada, Ireland, New Zealand, and South Africa). All other independent countries were handled through the Foreign Office.

5. Public Record Office, Group Air 2, Docket 3157 (Air Ministry files). Relevant correspondence copied and held by DHist. Sir Gerald Campbell to Dominions Office, September 13th, 1939.

6. Dominions Office to Campbell, September 26th, 1939. *Ibid.*

On October 15th a British delegation headed by Lord Riverdale and including Air Marshal Sir Christopher Courtney arrived in Ottawa to thrash out the details of the BCATP itself. Canadian attention was fixed firmly on the ramifications of undertaking such an ambitious training scheme. On the 16th the British High Commissioner summarized his most recent discussions with Prime Minister King:

> I have now received further letter (which I have shown to Riverdale and Courtney) from the Canadian Government dated the 14th October.
>
> While they have noted the United Kingdom Government proposal for the early formation of Royal Canadian Air Force squadron overseas and they desire this to be considered independently of the comprehensive Empire training scheme, Canadian Government say that the immediate despatch of even one unit would seriously detract from the inception and the development of training. It would entail . . . a Royal Headquarters [sic], a pool of officers, and a pool of airmen to replace wastage, as well as requiring constant flow of personnel from Canada as replacements.
>
> While, therefore, Canadian Government feel that "it is for many reasons desirable that Canada's contribution in the air should be recognized and confirmed by early participation of Royal Canadian Air Force units overseas," they consider "in view of most recent communications on the subject of training received from the United Kingdom" that Canadian participation in the form of an overseas squadron "at this stage should not now be contemplated."
>
> Canadian Government refer, however, to the suggestion that squadron might be provided from trained Canadian personnel now in the United Kingdom. They suggest that if the R.A.F. is prepared to form a squadron from the above personnel now in the R.A.F. and to maintain it so far as possible as unit manned by Canadians until training here produces flow of personnel from Canada and until the Royal Canadian Air Force can assume full commitments for this unit, then "the much to be desired recognition of Canadian participation will have been initiated." They add that as the Canadian contribution increases this squadron could be taken over as a Royal Canadian Air Force Squadron. . . .

Two typical groups of the young Canadians who joined the Royal Air Force in the 1930's. *Top:* En route to England in October 1938 are (*back row, l to r*) T.F. Kerr (Montreal), H.A.G. Smith (Kingston), E. Pollard (Montreal), A.C. Forsyth (Winnipeg), R.B. Fleming (Stellerton), P.S. Turner (Toronto), R.D. Grassick (London); (*front row, l to r*) F.W.B. Knapton (Vancouver), A.B. Parker (Winnipeg), A.I. Watterson (Ottawa), E.A. Allen (Ottawa), K.M. Laird (Montreal), and E.R. McGovern (Moncton).   (Una Grassick via Public Archives of Canada [PAC])

Bottom: (*front row, l to r*) G.W. Salzgerber, Graham C. Campbell, unknown, Ken G. Taylor, Frank Rogers, D.H. Howell; (*back row, l to r*) C.R. Tufford, W.E.N. Keller, Bud Robson, G.M. McCaw, Arthur Jackson, J.E. Monette, N.G. Crunna.   (C.I.R. Arthur)

One of the schools at which the Canadians learned to fly was 1 Elementary Flying Training School at Hatfield, operated by de Havilland Aircraft Company. The photo shows a lineup of this school's Tiger Moths. (Una Grassick via PAC)

Another Canadian recruit, Gary Madore, views a Hawker Hind Trainer. (A. Madore)

Training accidents were inevitable— here, the results of a taxiing accident between two Hart Trainers at Montrose in 1938. (C.I.R. Arthur)

Canadian pilots during advanced training at RAF Sealand, 1939. The aircraft
are Hart trainers. *Top*: (*l to r*): K.C. Forsythe (Winnipeg), K.M. Laird (Montreal), A.G. Egerton (Montreal), G.M. Stewart (London or Stratford), J. Shepherd (Victoria), H. Burns (Halifax), M.E. Pollard (Montreal), H.A.G. Smith
(Kingston), A. Edy (Winnipeg), R.D. Grassick (London). *Bottom*: (*foreground,
l to r*): A.C. Forsythe, H.A. G. Smith, R.D. Grassick, H. Burns, M.E. Pollard, J.
Shepherd, A.G. Egerton, K.M. Laird. G.M. Stewart (standing near nose). A.
Edy (looking into rear cockpit).   (photos courtesy Una Grassick via PAC)

R.D. Grassick by Hawker Hart Trainer at RAF Sealand, 1939.
(Una Grassick via PAC)

Original members of No. 242 Squadron, Royal Air Force, taken late February or early March, 1940. All are Canadians. (*Front row, l to r*): P/O N.K. Stansfeld, P/O L.E. Chambers, P/O R.D. Grassick, P/O R.H. Wiens, F/L D.R. Miller, S/L F.M. Gobeil (commanding officer), F/L J.L. Sullivan, P/O J.W. Graafstra, P/O P.S. Turner, P/O R.L. Hill, P/O J.W. Mitchell. (*Rear row, l to r*); P/O D.G. MacQueen, P/O H.L. Niccolls, P/O J.B. Latta, P/O M.K. Brown, P/O W.L. McKnight, P/O J.B. Smiley, P/O G.A. Madore, P/O J. Benzie, P/O W.A. Waterton. (Una Grassick via PAC)

No. 242 Squadron was initially equipped with Bristol Blenheim IF's. These were Blenheim light bombers converted to fighters by the addition of a pack with four machine guns beneath the fuselage. Above is a Blenheim I bomber at Montrose in 1938 (C.I.R. Arthur), and below P/O B. Smiley stands by one of No. 242's machines (Una Grassick via PAC).

On 9 December 1939 No. 242 Squadron was visited by a number of VIPs—the Hon. Vincent Massey (Canadian High Commissioner to Britain), the Hon. T.A. Crerar (Canadian Minister of Mines and Resources), AVM R.E. Saul (AOC No. 13 Group RAF), A/Cdre L.S. Breadner (RCAF), and W/C F.V. Heakes (RCAF Liaison Officer). In the top photo, posed against a Spitfire, are (l to r): W.L. McKnight, D.G. MacQueen, P.D. MacDonald (Adjutant), D.F. Jones, W/C Richardson (station commanding officer), J.B. Latta, J.B. Smiley, F.M. Gobeil, R. Coe, R.H. Wiens (just over Crerar's shoulder), Hon. T.A. Crerar, R.L. Hill, H.L. Niccolls, Hon. Vincent Massey, J.W. Mitchell, AVM Saul, M.K. Brown, D.R. Miller, A/Cdre L.S. Breadner, J.L. Sullivan, W/C F.V. Heakes, P.S. Turner, G.A. Madore. In the bottom photo are P/O's R.H. Wiens, W.A. Waterton, J.F. Howitt, F/O R. Coe, P/O Grassick, T.A. Crerar, P/O's H.L. Niccolls, D.F. Jones.   (photos courtesy Una Grassick via PAC)

Later on 9 December, Flying Officer Richard Coe and Hazel Browne were married. Tragically, Coe was killed one month later in a flying accident. In the bottom photo are (*l to r*): Macdonald (adj.), F/L Miller, F/O Chambers (between groom and bride), Mrs. Miller, S/L Gobeil.　　　　　(D.R. Miller)

By the end of February, No. 242 had been equipped with Hurricanes. Some of these aircraft form photo props for (*top left*) P/O G.A. Madore and P/O R.D. Grassick, (*top right*) F/L J. L. Sullivan and P/O Grassick, and (*bottom*) P/O's Madore, P.S. Turner, and Grassick. (Una Grassick via PAC)

Riverdale and Courtney agree with me that this answer misses the point as to the value of a token force as soon as possible. But I think that there is little hope of Canadian Government departing from the foregoing view.[7]

The last paragraph indicates that the British High Commissioner and his associates were not enthusiastic about the idea, but later that day they altered their views, accepting that a major RCAF overseas effort would cripple the BCATP at its birth, given the fact that the small pre-war RCAF would have to serve as nucleus for both programmes. A new point was raised; the formation of a Canadian squadron within the RAF

... would, if suitable publicity were given, have just as great propaganda value for use against the enemy as if personnel were specially despatched from Canada for this purpose.[8]

So far as they affected the history of No. 242 Squadron, Sir Gerald Campbell and the Dominions Office had served their purpose; they had conveyed to British authorities the fact that Canada was not likely to despatch an RCAF squadron overseas in the near future, but that the Canadian leaders wished to have some national presence overseas, even if it were an RAF unit manned largely by Canadians already enrolled in that force. As a matter of routine, the major communications between Sir Gerald and the Dominions Office were passed to the Foreign Office. It was there that the idea really caught fire, and for the most curious reasons.

The Foreign Office seized upon one point Sir Gerald Campbell had raised—the value of a CAN/RAF squadron in terms of propaganda directed against the enemy—and took it one step further. On October 18th a Foreign Office Official wrote:

The presence of a Canadian Royal Air Force squadron in France would be most helpful so far as French public opinion is concerned as it would be regarded as a clear indication that an expeditionary force will be sent by Canada. Whether this Canadian Royal Air Force squadron is made up of Canadians who have just come from Canada or Canadians

---

7. *Ibid.* This document also appears in Foreign Office records, Public Records Office, Group FO 371, Docket 23966 (copies held by DHist).

8. *Ibid.*

already in the Royal Air Force would not seem to matter much so long as they are Canadians and are in a squadron called the Royal Canadian Air Force. The more French Canadians there are in such a squadron the better. Perhaps it might be thought desirable to point out the propaganda value of this squadron in France to the Dominions Office and the War Office.[9]

This view of a possible Canadian squadron touched off a round of memos, minutes, and telephone conversations between Dominions Office and Foreign Office personnel. By October 20th the two organizations had agreed upon the desirability of such a move, and were resolved to place the idea before the Air Ministry, the department that would ultimately be responsible for the unit, regardless of what motives inspired its conception.[10] An added spur came on October 26th, when Sir Gerald Campbell telegraphed his superiors, urging "immediate approval" of an RAF squadron composed of Canadians, it being of "great political importance in the Dominion."[11] The Air Ministry agreed at once; on October 27th a message was on its way to Sir Gerald, stating the general terms under which the squadron would be formed:

> ... we suggest that one of new Fighter Squadrons now about to form should be composed as far as possible of Canadian-born personnel. A Squadron Leader and a complete squadron of pilots are immediately available but not many of the necessary tradesmen. This would be better than withdrawing Canadian personnel from other squadrons which would involve extensive postings as well as loss of efficiency. We suggest squadron should be called Number Blank (Canadian) Squadron, R.A.F. until Royal Canadian Air Force assumes full commitments. The squadron earmarked, subject

9. *Ibid*.

10. *Ibid*. The Foreign Office concern with impressing French public opinion must be understood in the light of Anglo-French relations at that time. France had entered the war reluctantly and entertained hopes for a negotiated peace now that Germany had seemingly settled its "Polish problem". Britain was anxious to instill some military enthusiasm in her ally. See William L. Shirer, *The Collapse of the Third Republic* (London, 1970), chapters 26 and 27.

11. Sir Gerald Campbell to Dominions Office, October 36th, 1939. See note 5.

to concurrence of Canadian Government, is No. 242 Squadron which is about to form at Church Fenton.[12]

Without waiting for Canadian approval, the Royal Air Force proceeded to act on this policy statement. No. 242 (Canadian) Squadron was formally born on October 30th, 1939, at Church Fenton, Yorkshire, half-way between Leeds and York. The number perpetuated an earlier and rather undistinguished unit which had been formed in August 1918 to fly Short 184 seaplanes, and had been disbanded in May 1919. Canadian concurrence in the organization of No. 242 was not transmitted to Britain until November 16th. Even then Canadian authorities sought to have the unit redesignated "No. 3 (Fighter) Squadron, Royal Canadian Air Force", a change Air Ministry resisted because there was already a No. 3 Squadron in the RAF.[13]

No. 242 remained a paper formation until November 1st, when Squadron Leader Fowler Morgan Gobeil arrived at Church Fenton to take charge. A native of Ottawa, Gobeil had entered the Royal Military College, Kingston, in 1927; two years later he had been commissioned as a Pilot Officer in the RCAF. He had subsequently flown as a member of the RCAF's *Siskin* aerobatic team, making him one of the few members of the force in the 1930's to have any type of experience on fighter aircraft. An articulate staff officer, he had been promoted to Squadron Leader in April 1939. Gobeil had been despatched to the United Kingdom on an exchange posting that summer. He was now assigned to the "Canadian" squadron—whether at RAF or RCAF initiative is uncertain—serving as the official channel between No. 242 Squadron and RCAF authorities. At least one such link would be needed as long as No. 242 constituted a potential RCAF unit.

Gobeil's posting has been attended by some confustion. He had first been informed that he was to take over No. 2 Squadron, RAF. On checking further he had discovered that No. 2, an Army Co-operation unit, was stationed in France. This he had found puz-

12. *Ibid.*

13. *Ibid.* It is not known why Canadian authorities wanted to call it No. 3 (Fighter) Squadron; they may have been thinking of the two-squadron Canadian Air Force formed in England in 1918, regarding the new unit as a continuation of that short-lived force. RAF objections were understandable, though they were not raised when No. 1 (RCAF) Squadron was sent to Britain in June 1940.

zling, for he could scarcely imagine that the RAF would hand him responsibility for one of their units in the field. Three days passed, during which his household was in pandemonium, before a correction came through. Even after assuming his duties, Gobeil was uncertain of their significance. In a letter to a colleague he wrote;

> At present we have no aircraft. Apparently we are to get a number of young P/Os from Training Pools and will have to push them through to squadron efficiency. In that respect it looks as though this posting is a continuation of my training interchange programme. I certainly hope that I get a posting to as many types of squadrons as possible, so as to cover all phases of training.[14]

Even though it was his first substantive command, Gobeil was not informed of his mandate for some time. It was finally spelled out to him on November 21st in a letter from Wing Commander F.V. Heakes, RCAF Liaison Officer, London. This stated clearly what Canadian authorities expected of the unit:

> Further to my wires with respect to the organization of your unit, you will no doubt be interested to learn that this unit was formed at the suggestion of the Canadian authorities in order that Canada may have early participation in the war.
>
> The intention is that it shall be manned by pilots of Canadian birth at present in the R.A.F. It is possible that later it may become a R.C.A.F. unit.
>
> There is considerable political significance attached to the formation of this unit; therefore we are most anxious to be informed fully of what is transpiring.[15]

On November 3rd two Flight Commanders were posted to No. 242 Squadron—Flight Lieutenant Donald Robert Miller (a native of Saskatoon) and Flight Lieutenant John Lewis Sullivan (born in Smith Falls, Ontario and raised in Guelph). Both men had

14. *Hitchins Papers* held by DHist, Reference 75/514 (File F.1), covering No. 242 Squadron. Letter from Squadron Leader Gobeil to Wing Commander F.V. Heakes, November 4th, 1939.

15. Chronological File, RCAF Liaison Officer, London, England. Held by DHist (reference 181.009 D.1843).

sailed to England on their own initiative and had joined the RAF in March 1936; Miller had been walking the streets of London with less than four pounds in his pocket on the day he was informed of his acceptance. After initial and advanced training they had gone to fighter squadrons—Sullivan to No. 43 (Hawker *Furies* and then *Hurricanes*), Miller to No. 64 (Hawker *Demons*, converting to Bristol *Blenheims* in December 1938). Sullivan had actually fired his guns in earnest during the war; on September 17th, 1939, while still with No. 43 Squadron, he had shot down a British barrage balloon that had broken from its moorings and was presenting a hazard to air traffic.

The first tasks assigned to Miller and Sullivan were instructional. In the weeks that followed they would initiate the junior pilots into the intricacies of the many aircraft types assigned to No. 242. "Dual instruction" was to be their most frequent logbook entry, interspersed with occasional short trips to pick up new training machines.[16]

The real flow of pilots began on November 5th with the arrival of Flying Officer John William Graafstra (Souris, Manitoba), who became a Deputy Flight Commander. He had originally travelled to England to study music, but had changed his mind and applied for an RAF Short Service Commission that had been granted in January 1937. Graafstra was accompanied by Pilot Officer Robert Davidson Grassick (London, Ontario), soon to be known as "Slim", because he was not, or "Jumbo", as his girth increased.

The next day brought a veritable flood of aircrew—Flying Officer Lorne Edward Chambers (Vernon, British Columbia), who came from flying *Spitfires* with No. 74 Squadron, plus Pilot Officers Marvin Kitchener Brown (Kincardine, Ontario), Arthur Henry Deacon (Invermay, Saskatchewan), Dale Fred Jones (Dinsmore, Saskatchewan), John Blandford Latta (Victoria), William Lidstone McKnight (Edmonton-born but Calgary-raised), Donald Garfield McQueen (High River, Alberta), Garfield Alexander Madore (Fort William, Ontario), James William Mitchell (Kirkfield, Ontario), Hugh Leslie Niccolls (Rosetown, Saskatchewan), Joseph Beverly Smiley (Wolseley, Saskatchewan), and Russell Henry Wiens (Jansen,

16. Logbook of D.R. Miller, loaned to the author. Sullivan's logbook is not available, but presumably its contents differed little from Miller's.

Saskatchewan).

The same day, November 6th, the squadron also acquired an Adjutant (administrative officer). Pilot Officer Peter Drummond MacDonald, a native of Halifax, Nova Scotia, had gone overseas in 1915 with the 85th Battalion, Canadian Expeditionary Force. He had subsequently served in France, been wounded, and won a commission. MacDonald had remained in England after the war, completed his legal studies, and had been admitted to the Bar. Since 1924 he had been Conservative Member of Parliament for the Isle of Wight; since 1937 he had also been a member of the Royal Air Force Volunteer Reserve. MacDonald continued to sit as an MP while on duty with the RAF—a curious position and the subject of comment by at least one historian.[17]

There were more pilots to come. On November 7th Flying Officer Richard Coe of Winfield, British Columbia, reported to the squadron. He had obtained his RAF Short Service Commission in December 1936 and came to No. 242 with *Hurricane* experience gained in No. 56 Squadron. Finally, on November 20th, three further aircrew reported—Pilot Officers James Francis Howitt (Guelph, Ontario), Percival Stanley Turner (Toronto), and William Albert Waterton (Edmonton-born, but raised in Camrose, Alberta). By the end of the month No. 242 had its full complement of pilots and 178 groundcrew.

Most of the pilots were fresh out of flying school, the logical consequence of the RAF's reluctance to switch experienced Canadian pilots out of existing squadrons. Nobody had the least combat time, not even from an Imperial "brushfire" war. Although it had been formed as much for propaganda as for operational purposes, the existence of the "Canadian" squadron was not revealed to the press until December 1st, 1939. The timing and wording of the press release had been the subject of several trans-Atlantic telegrams between Ottawa and London. It proved to be a misleading report, stating that the squadron included personnel from all provinces, and

17. See Chapter 5, note 7. The duties of an Adjutant were very broad. The post was intended to relieve Commanding Officers of petty or routine duties so that they might concentrate on larger matters or operations. Responsible for stores, accounting, and records, the Adjutant was also the "ears and eyes" of his commander, reporting any irregularities to him. With such tasks, it is evident that Adjutants would have a significant effect upon the squadron.

suggesting that No. 242 was about to become a front-line unit—at a time when it possessed not a single combat aircraft![18] This impression was heightened when Sir Kingsley Wood (Secretary of State for Air) declared in Britain's House of Commons that the unit was "about to take its place in the first line of air defence of this country".[19]

The original pilots of No. 242 Squadron represented a random selection of Canadian life, yet their backgrounds said much about the forces that had brought them to this corner of Yorkshire. Their average age was 23—a bit older than was usual in fighter squadrons later in the war—and they represented five of the nine Canadian provinces at that date—British Columbia, Alberta, Saskatchewan, Manitoba, and Ontario. Their ranks included one career officer (Gobeil), who shared with Waterton the distinction of having attended Royal Military College. The latter had entered RMC in 1935 and was commissioned in the Alberta Dragoons, a Militia unit, in 1937. After leaving RMC he had been employed as a physical fitness instructor in an Alberta youth training programme before heading for England to join the RAF. Other occupations included a former RCMP special constable (Sullivan), an ex-salmon fisherman (Latta), a bank clerk (Graafstra), a former hardware merchant, hockey player, and band leader (Deacon), a medical student (McKnight, who had switched to flying but hoped to continue his studies at Edinburgh after the war), a former life guard (Turner), a dairyman (Howitt), a hardrock gold miner (Smiley), a grain elevator operator (Weins), and a civil engineer (Niccolls). Mitchell was following a short family tradition; his father had served in the Royal Flying Corps during the First World War.

They had come to the Royal Air Force at different times but in roughly similar circumstances. Most had obtained Private Pilot's Licenses in Canada before going to Britain. Madore had been taught by his older brother Andy, an instructor with the Saskatoon Flying Club when the family had been residing in that city; he had also

18. For example see "Assign Unit of Fighters to Defence", Toronto *Globe and Mail*, December 2nd, 1939, reprinting a Canadian Press despatch dated December 1st. Most Canadian daily papers carried virtually the same report under varying headlines.

19. *Parliamentary Debates* (London, 1939), December 12th, 1939, p. 1070.

learned some technical details while working at the Canadian Car and Foundry aircraft plant in Fort William. The more experienced members (Miller, Sullivan, Graafstra, Coe, and Chambers) had gone to Britain entirely at their own expense, with no guarantees of being accepted by the RAF. Since 1934 the RCAF had been screening candidates for the RAF, conducting interviews and medical examinations. This programme had been expanded in 1938-39, in which fiscal year 118 Canadians had been sent to England under the "Direct Entry Scheme". Thus, most of the junior members of No. 242 had gone overseas in circumstances where they could reasonably expect to be recruited quickly.

There were exceptions and special cases. John Latta had enjoyed the special patronage of Captain H. Seymour-Biggs, a retired English mariner residing in Victoria. An enthusiastic amateur recruiter, this gentleman had assisted dozens of Canadian youths to join the RAF during the late 1930's. He had handled much of their paperwork, arranged medical tests, provided references and letters of introduction, and occasionally had advanced them travel funds. These were "Seymour-Biggs boys"; they kept in close touch with their patron whose name was frequently mentioned in newspaper accounts of their adventures. Unfortunately, he was not fully informed about some RAF training policies, and some young men reached England with unrealistic hopes of becoming pilots only to be diverted to groundcrew training.

Gary Madore's route to No. 242 had been as difficult as Latta's had been simple. RCAF officers had not been encouraging, but in 1938 he had sailed to England with the hope of joining the RAF. His application was not accepted immediately and the delay taxed his financial resources. His brother Andy sent him $75.00, assuring him that passage money home would be available if needed. That was not needed; Madore was accepted by the force a few weeks later.[20]

The pilots of No. 242 Squadron had, to some degree, been joining the RAF in batches. Turner and Grassick had come over on the same boat and had been appointed Acting Pilot Officers on Probation on the same date, January 14th, 1939. Deacon, McKnight, and Mitchell had won similar appointments on April 15th, followed by Latta on April 24th. Brown, Hill, Jones, MacQueen, Madore,

20. A.F. Madore to the author, September 20th, 1980.

Niccolls, Smiley, and Wiens had gained entry on May 13th; Howitt and Waterton were last on June 10th, 1939. Now, with less than a year's instruction behind them, and their flying badges newly sewn on, they prepared to become fighter pilots.

No. 242's pilots were all Canadians, but the situation with respect to groundcrew was markedly different. At the outset the tradesmen were entirely British. On December 22nd, 1939, Sir Gerald Campbell received a report on the status of groundcrew "Canadianization" which also indicated RAF policy intentions respecting the unit:

> At the present moment the ground personnel is British, but it is proposed to replace British airmen by any Canadian ground personnel there may be serving at present with other R.A.F. units. The intention of course is that the squadron will be converted into a R.C.A.F. squadron when the ground personnel become predominantly Canadian.[21]

Air Ministry strove to provide as many Canadian tradesmen as possible, "combing" other units for some and posting several others directly to No. 242 from trades courses. A few were found to be unsuitable and returned to their original units, but by the early spring of 1940 roughly sixty Canadian groundcrew had made their way into the squadron.[22]

As with the pilots, the tradesmen had reached the RAF by a variety of routes. Typical of these was Leading Aircraftman Robert Emery Sabourin. Born in Calgary and raised on the Pacific coast, he had attempted to join the RCAF in 1937, but had been turned down owing to a shortage of vacancies. Nevertheless, Sabourin had impressed several officers who provided him with recommendations when he applied to the RAF. After passing a medical examination at Esquimault he was accepted by the British, sailed to Liverpool in January 1938, and went directly to the School of Technical Training at Halton where he became an Armourer. Sabourin was posted to No. 242 Squadron in March 1940; he would remain with the unit until September 1941.

21. See note 5.

22. Much information on Canadian groundcrew has been provided by Albert W. Taylor of Vancouver, a former tradesman with No. 242 who has maintained close ties with members of the squadron.

The Canadian pilots had a relaxed rapport with groundcrew, especially those who had also come from the Dominion. Some pilots and tradesmen had attended the same schools. Many of the "erks" had travelled to Britain hoping to receive pilot training, and a few still entertained ambitions of remustering to aircrew. Nevertheless, the service lifestyle of the officers differed markedly from that of "the troops".

The Canadian airmen endured the same spartan conditions as their British colleagues. At bases like Church Fenton they lived in barracks, 30 to a room, each man allotted 60 square feet of floor space. Furnishings consisted of steel lockers for personal effects plus wooden stands. They slept on three-piece mattresses called "biscuits", while the hot water heating systems struggled against the damp English climate. Pay was not generous. Depending on his trade grouping, a Leading Aircraftman daily drew between four shillings (for, say, a parachute packer or telephone operator) and five shillings six pence (for skilled armourers, airframe or engine fitters, instrument repairers, or wireless mechanics). For the duration of the war all non-commissioned ranks eventually earned an additional six pence per day.

Junior officers, aircrew included, had more comfortable accommodation—two men to a small but well furnished room. The Commanding Officer and Flight Commanders, being married, lived off the base in pleasant cottages; Miller's wife was adept at cooking over the open hearth of their house. Batmen (civilians or airmen acting as servants) waited upon the officers; Gobeil was entitled to one; the other pilots had one batman for every three officers. Basic pay for a Pilot Officer was 14 shillings six pence per day, for a Flying Officer 18 shillings six pence per day, and for a Flight Lieutenant one pound one shilling nine pence per day. Married personnel living off the base were granted modest accommodation allowances.

Whatever their trades or ranks, the Canadians shared a common opinion of English food—at least that found in RAF messes. It was dreadful, and the memory of it lingers after four decades. Years later James Howitt would recall, "We were barbarians to the English types; we covered everything we ate with Heinz ketchup". To this a former tradesman, L.H. Stopforth, has added, "English food pretty well *had* to be covered with ketchup to make it palatable". A greasy brown stew seems to have been the mess specialty at Church Fenton. Vegetables were boiled until they were devoid of flavour, then smothered in sweet sauces. Noel Stansfeld remembers treacle tarts—rather like hockey pucks with a syrupy sauce. It appears that the food improved later in the war, particularly in those messes that employed Italian prisoners-of-war as cooks!

The Canadians of all ranks introduced one piece of North American culture to Britain. In good weather they played baseball, taught the game to their English comrades, and travelled to other airfields for matches. British spectators were numerous and interested, although they understood the game scarcely better than the Canadians understood cricket.

Squadron training began in November using three *Magisters*, a *Harvard*, and a *Battle*. Word soon got around that plans were afoot to equip the unit with *Battles*. The prospect of going to war in these sluggish light bombers was not to the pilots' liking. On November 15, when Air Vice Marshal R.E. Saul (Air Officer Commanding, No. 13 Group) visited No. 242, he asked each pilot what type of aircraft he would like to fly. In every instance the reply was "Spitfires!". Saul was amused and promised to see if the request could be met. One can imagine the disappointment that followed when seven *Blenheim IF's* arrived in December, together with three more *Battles*.[23]

Typical of the training conducted at this period was the experience of Pilot Officer Howitt. His first flight with the squadron was on November 20th in a *Magister* (R1824) with Flight Lieutenant Sullivan at the controls. On the 23rd he spent an hour flying solo, doing circuits and landings. Howitt made two flights on the 24th and two on the 27th, totalling two hours 20 minutes, which were described as "local flying"—familiarization with the countryside around Church Fenton. Further *Magister* hops—"instrument flying" —followed with Turner, Jones, Latta, Mitchell, and Madore. On the 30th he went up in the *Harvard* (P5865) with Sullivan (40 minutes,

---

23. Stan Turner has told this writer that No. 242 Squadron was also issued two or three *Gladiator* biplane fighters which were reserved for experienced pilots; the statement is repeated by him in print. See "No Horsing", *Airforce*, September 1980, p. 21. The squadron diary does not mention them, and the excellent Air Britain Publications series on RAF aircraft compiled by James J. Halley (see Bibliography) lists no *Gladiators* as having been on the strength of No. 242. With all due respect to Turner's distinguished record, it seems that on this and several other points his memory is off the mark. The *Gladiators* he recalls may have been assigned to the station, or to another unit at Church Fenton.

dual instruction) and then flew it solo for half an hour. He continued to fly the "Maggie" and *Harvard* into December, being introduced to the *Blenheim* on the 19th (L6792) and the *Battle* on the 31st (L5014 and L5406).[24]

In the meantime, No. 242 was fulfilling its public relations function. During Air Vice Marshal Saul's November visit, a Squadron Leader Ward had come as well, acting as Press Officer to get the unit into British and Canadian papers. On December 9th there was another visit by "brass"—Saul once more, accompanied by the Honourable Vincent Massey (Canadian High Commissioner to Britain), the Honourable Thomas A. Crerar (Canadian Minister of Mines and Resources), Mr. C.W. Jackson (an aide to Crerar), Air Commodore Lloyd Breadner, and Wing Commander F.V. Heakes. No. 242 was paraded for the occasion while assorted Canadian and British reporters looked on.

The visit produced a considerable amount of publicity back home, particularly through Canadian Press despatches filed by Edwin S. Johnson.[25] Western papers would later carry a six-part "human interest" series of articles about the squadron by Francis Stevens.[26] Some reporting was very muddled. A Canadian Press story suggested that No. 242 was an experienced outfit, declaring, "Most of the boys have already taken part in air duels against enemy raiders".[27] Pilot Officer Jones was described as a combat veteran in the Saskatchewan papers,[28] and a photograph of Flying Officer Coe was captioned as showing him "standing on the wing of his fighting plane"—a *Magister*![29]

24. Howitt logbook, viewed by the author April 1980.

25. See for example "Canadian Squadron Eager for Air Fight", Winnipeg *Free Press*, January 2nd, 1940.

26. The series was carried by the Winnipeg *Free Press*, Regina *Leader Post*, and Saskatoon *Star-Phoenix*, January 20th, 22nd, 23rd, 24th, 25th, and 26th, 1940.

27. "Canadian Minister Meets Youthful Canadian Flyers", Hamilton *Spectator*, December 9th, 1939.

28. Saskatoon *Star-Phoenix*, December 18th, 1939; Regina *Leader Post*, December 21st, 1939.

29. Vancouver *Sun*, January 12th, 1940.

One of the reporters was Matthew Halton, who subsequently filed an account glowing with the moving prose that was to make him famous. Much of his despatch was naive, a reflection of his unfamiliarity with air force subjects and of No. 242's nature as a unit of novices. There were *Spitfires* present on the "mist-wrapped" English field, and Halton assumed that the Canadians were already flying them. He queried Stan Turner about their handling qualities; Turner sidestepped the questions (which the reporter attributed to modesty) by turning the conversation to other matters. Halton did catch one sentiment that was honest enough—the keenness of the pilots to see action. "We are dying for this war to start", they declared.[30]

On the afternoon of December 9th the squadron celebrated a social event. Dick Coe married Pauline Hazel Browne of Kelowna, British Columbia. The bride and groom had been apart for two years, and she had arrived in England only two weeks before. "Some say we are foolish to marry now," said Coe, "but we have considered everything." Gobeil gave the bride away while Lorne Chambers acted as best man. The pilots toasted the couple, unaware of impending tragedy.

The visit of the Canadian delegation indicated the continued official interest in No. 242 Squadron. Over the holiday season this was shown in less formal ways. At Christmas and New Year the High Commissioner entertained unit personnel at meals featuring oysters, stuffed turkey, mince pies, and delicacies prepared by a French chef. An orchestra played during these meals, and the men were also treated to London shows.[31]

When not flying the *Blenheims*, *Battles*, and *Magisters*, Squadron Leader Gobeil and his pilots had much to do. There were lectures to attend on air force organization, aircraft recognition, engines, tactics, signals, rigging, armament, battle orders, radio equipment, navigational aids, plus revolver practice and "flying" in the Link Trainer. Elsewhere, behind the scenes, No. 242 Squadron was the subject of official head-scratching by the RAF and wire-pulling by Canadian officials. Exactly what role should it be assigned?

30. "Dying for War to Start", Toronto *Daily Star*, December 9th, 1939.

31. Toronto *Globe and Mail*, December 26th, 1939.

And in accordance with that role, what aircraft should it be issued?

On that point Gobeil had no doubts. He had taken Air Vice Marshal Saul's remarks of November 15th to be a commitment that No. 242 would be a day fighter unit with *Spitfires*. He had not been disturbed at receiving additional *Battles*; that type, with its Merlin engine and retractable undercarriage, was commonly used to prepare pilots for high performance fighters. The *Blenheims* had been a different matter. On November 23rd, even before they arrived, Gobeil wrote to the RCAF Liaison Office, vigorously protesting such a development. He stressed that Canada's aerial reputation had been built upon the exploits of single-seater fighter pilots of the First World War and went on to declare that making No. 242 a *Blenheim* unit would defeat the aim of firing the public imagination. He was advised to take the matter up with Saul; simultaneously RCAF authorities undertook to lobby on behalf of No. 242 for equipment more in keeping with national aspirations and traditions.[32]

The problem was resolved on December 15th by an anonymous official in Air Ministry who was wrestling with the question of allocating ten new squadrons to various duties, including convoy protection, night defence, and day defence. His memo is worth quoting at length, for it shows that the pressure applied by Gobeil and his superiors had been effective. Moreover, the document demonstrates that other possibilities had now entered the picture, such as attaching No. 242 to a Canadian Army contingent which might be sent to France:

> The selection of the two squadrons to be re-equipped with Hurricanes for the defence of Scapa is complicated by the necessity to consider carefully the future role of the Canadian Fighter Squadron. The Canadian Squadron would resent being equipped with Blenheims when British Squadrons had Hurricanes and Spitfires. It is therefore desirable to give them 8-gun fighters. A further consideration which must be borne in mind is that it will probably be found desirable to send the Canadian Squadron to France to help in the defence of the Canadian contingent. We should therefore avoid arming the squadron with Spitfires since we do not want to send Spitfires to France. It therefore follows that the Cana-

32. Gobeil to Heakes, November 23rd, 1939; Heakes to Gobeil, November 27th, 1939; cable from RCAF Liaison Office to RCAF Headquarters, Ottawa, November 30th, 1939. See note 14.

dian Squadron should be equipped with Hurricanes.

It seems that the best way to do this will be to give No. 242 (the Canadian Squadron) and No. 253 Hurricanes. In February 1940 when the two Hurricane Squadrons are due to go north for the defence of Scapa, No. 242 should go to France in exchange for one Field Force Hurricane Squadron which will return to England and go to Wick with No. 253.[33]

"Scapa", of course, was Scapa Flow, the great British naval base in the Orkney Islands north of Scotland. Beyond that, some explanations may be in order. Keeping *Spitfires* out of France was a policy dictated by two factors—the need to standardize on one fighter type in the field and the ruggedness of the forward airfields in France, most of which would have reduced any squadron equipped with *Spitfires* (notorious for their delicate undercarriages) to a collection of spare parts.

One might ask why such an elaborate shuffle was required, with No. 242 Squadron going to the Continent and another squadron coming back to Britain. Could the unit not have re-inforced RAF formations already there? Upon the outbreak of war the RAF had despatched twenty-seven squadrons to France, including six fighter squadrons. They had swamped the bases assigned to them, and in the harsh winter that followed plans to upgrade and expand the airfield network had to be shelved. Some qualitative changes were made early in 1940, trading a pair of *Battle* squadrons off in return for *Blenheim* units and converting two *Gladiator* squadrons to *Hurricanes*. The only way No. 242 could be accommodated would be to have it trade places with a unit already there.

Late in December the welcome news reached No. 242 that it was to receive *Hurricanes*. The pilots' experience on the *Battles* would be useful, both types being powered by Merlin engines. On January 5th, having returned from New Year's leave, Squadron Leader Gobeil and five others proceeded to St. Athan, South Wales, to pick up the first lot of fighters. All had some degree of experience on the type, though some checks had to be run before they could take delivery of the aircraft. On the 10th they set out for Ternhill, en route to their base. Unhappily, they ran into weather far worse than had been forecast. The newly-married Flying Officer Coe, while attempting to force-land at Appleton (near Warrington, Lanca-

33. See note 5.

shire), crashed and was killed—No. 242's first fatality. Gobeil came down at Culceth, near Padgate, a few miles away, and overturned as he landed. Fortunately, he was unhurt. Pilot Officer Grassick found Ringway aerodrome near Manchester and landed safely. Flight Lieutenant Sullivan, Flying Officer Graafstra, and Pilot Officer Turner reached Ternhill without mishap.

The weather remained poor; it was not until January 16th that an attempt was made to complete delivery of the first *Hurricanes*. On that day Sullivan, Grassick, and Turner took off from Ternhill. Once again the forecasts proved inaccurate. Encountering a severe cold front near Castleford (southeast of Leeds), all three had to make forced landings, Grassick near Wakefield (south of Leeds), Turner at Finningly (near Doncaster), and Sullivan still further south, at Hucknall (near Nottingham).[34]

It was, indeed, a foul winter, one of the worst on record. There had not been so much snowfall in forty years. For nineteen days all flying was washed out, making delivery of any aircraft impossible.[35] Pilots concentrated on ground training, and frequently joined the airmen in clearing snow from the runways, using ordinary shovels for lack of better equipment. Finally, on February 10th, the skies cleared. Ferrying began again; by the evening of the 12th the squadron possessed twelve new *Hurricanes*, and pilots were rushing

34. The account of this ill-starred operation is taken from No. 242's Operational Record Book. Turner's recollections of the events are somewhat different, and have been described in print; see note 23. His published account includes a spectacular crash in which he wrote off the *Hurricane*. On at least two points, however, he is wrong. He mentions that one of the ferry pilots was McKnight; that pilot, according to his logbook, did not fly *Hurricanes* until February. Turner also insists that the aircraft were all lost in the first flight, whereas there were two stages involved. Oddly, none of the crashes, including those involving Coe, Gobeil, or Turner, can be traced through Air Britain publications of the L-, N-, and P- series of aircraft.

35. Such is the account as given in the Squadron Operational Record Book, and confirmed by the Howitt logbook. The logbook of Flight Lieutenant Miller contains two entries that suggest one *Hurricane* might have been delivered before the weather closed down flying; on January 20th, 1940 he recorded one hour in *Hurricane* N2342, describing this as "Experience on type". On February 9th he flew the same machine for an hour and wrote "First flight on type". The two entries are puzzling in that they contradict each other as well as the Squadron ORB.

One of No. 242's Hurricanes warms up. P/O J.B. Smiley in front of wing and
F/L D.R. Miller near tail.   (D.R. Miller)

P/O J.W. Graafstra and P/O G.A. Madore.
                    (Una Grassick via National
                    Museums of Canada [NMC])

P/O R.H. Wiens by his Hurricane.   (D.R. Miller)

F/O Lorne Chambers taxiing in a Hurricane and photographed beside No. 242's LE.F, serial L1572. Note that both aircraft have the two-bladed wooden propeller characteristic of early Hurricanes.   (D.R. Miller)

Left: An early morning shot of (*l to r*), P/O's D.F. Jones, J.B. Smiley, and a pilot identified only as Clarke. Shortly after this photo was taken, Jones was killed in action and Smiley was taken prisoner of war.

(Una Grassick via NMC)

Two photos of Hurricane LE.H, serial N2320 with, above right, a battery cart in the foreground. This aircraft was lost in action during the fighting in France, May 1940. (A.W. Taylor)

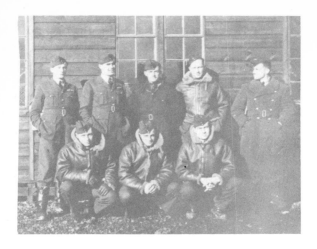

A group of No. 242 Sqdn pilots, in the spring of 1940. (*Front row, l to r*): P/O's W.L. McKnight, J.B. Smiley, D.G. MacQueen. (*Back row*): P/O R.H. Wiens, F/L D.R. Miller, P/O's M.K. Brown, N.K. Stansfeld, W.A. Waterton. (D.R. Miller)

F/L D.R. Miller with a Yorkshire bobby, May 1940. (D.R. Miller)

Two of No. 242's invaluable groundcrew, E.T. Cameron of New Glasgow, Nova Scotia, and G.Tyler of Sudbury, Ontario. (A.W. Taylor)

The parade square at RAF Church Fenton, No. 242's first station.

(A. W. Taylor)

Hurricane LE.G, serial L1972 at Church Fenton. (A.W. Taylor)

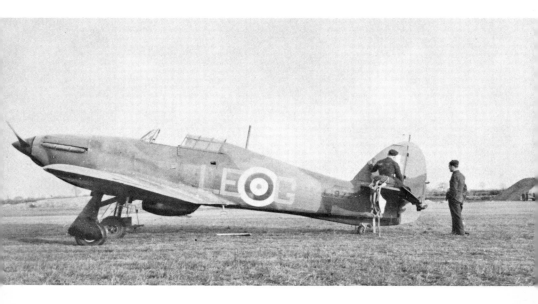

No. 242 Squadron airmen waiting to fly to France, May 1940.   (A.W. Taylor)

The Junkers *Ju 52* airliner of the Belgian Airline SABENA that flew No. 242
Sqdn groundcrew to France, May 1940.   (A.W. Taylor)

No. 242's first victories were scored against **Henschel** *Hs 126* army cooperation aircraft similar to the one depicted.　　　　　(Imperial War Museum [IWM])

Hurricane LE.A at Biggin Hill during the period No. 242 was flying from this station on operations over France.　　　　　(A.W. Taylor)

No. 242 Sqdn Hurricanes during the brief time the squadron operated from
Biggin Hill.   (A.W. Taylor)

to qualify on the type.

During this period of forced inactivity, two further pilots had joined No. 242, both reporting on February 3rd. Pilot Officers John Benzie of Winnipeg and Noel Karl Stansfeld of Vancouver were newly-trained and fresh from the Pilots' Pool. Both men had been granted RAF Short Service Commissions on June 24th, 1939. Here the similarity between the two good-looking pilots ended. They had come to the RAF for widely different reasons. Benzie had long been interested in the military, having been an army cadet for five years and a member of the Princess Patricia's Canadian Light Infantry for three. He had been attracted to the air force by a friend, Arthur R. Grevstad, who had earlier enlisted in the RAF. Stansfeld had knocked about in the mid-1930's, working for Standard Oil and as a stock broker besides prospecting near Yale, British Columbia. He looked upon the RAF as a good career prospect and had left Vancouver with $75.00. At Ottawa he had been interviewed by RCAF officers, recommended to the RAF, and given passage money to Britain. Arriving there, he had been assigned almost immediately to pilot training. [36]

It would appear that other Canadians had been attempting to secure transfers to No. 242. Such requests for specific postings would normally go through RAF channels, but on some occasions correspondence was directed to the RCAF Liaison Office in London. The staff there could only advise the people concerned to seek transfers through their own Commanding Officers. [37]

The training programme intensified with the delivery of the *Hurricanes*. Apart from occasional games of squash and sporadic trips to London, pilots and groundcrew alike were tied up with getting the unit operational.

Howitt's logbook illustrates the routine that was followed by the pilots. In January 1940 he had recorded eight hours and five minutes in the air, mostly in *Battles*, but the bad weather had stop-

36. Biographical details from Winnipeg *Tribune*, May 28th and June 5th, 1940, Winnipeg *Free Press*, September 24th, 1940, Vancouver *Sun*, July 19th, October 4th, and November 2nd, 1940, and from interview with N.K. Stansfeld, November 20th, 1980.

37. Wing Commander F.V. Heakes to A/Sergeant G.F. Cook, Biggin Hill, December 6th, 1939. See note 14.

ped all flying after January 22nd. On February 12th, however, with the *Hurricanes* arriving, he was given forty minutes of dual instruction in a *Harvard*, to re-acquaint him with high-powered single seater aircraft. The next day, following another forty minutes in the *Harvard*, he was allowed to take a *Hurricane* up for half an hour. By the 16th he had logged five hours and forty minutes on the type, all in "local flying".

Once he had mastered the *Hurricane*, Howitt joined his fellow pilots in formation flying, practicing radio telephone procedures at the same time. Next came tactical exercises—No. 1 Attack, No. 2 Attack, No. 3 Attack, battle climbs to 20,000 and 26,000 feet, and firing at towed targets.[38]

Air Ministry had instructed that No. 242 was to be operational for day and night operations by March 12th, if weather was particularly favourable, or by March 21st otherwise. This had led the pilots to expect a squadron movement to the Continent; the January 18th entry in the unit's diary contains a jubilant, "FRANCE FOR EASTER". Yet that goal was to elude them, for the delayed delivery of the *Hurricanes* and the frequent storms had curtailed the early part of the flying programme. Time was needed to practice operational procedures, and to get the guns properly harmonized. Night flying training began on February 29th and soon brought about the unit's second fatality. Just before dawn of March 3rd, while flying L2002, Pilot Officer Niccolls crashed and was killed near Bolton Percy, Tadcaster, Yorkshire. The *Hurricane* apparently flew into the ground at full speed, shedding wings, tailplanes, fin, and rear fuselage before halting and burning. A little less than a month before, on February 5th, Niccolls had been featured in a radio broadcast to Canada, describing the activities of No. 242.[39]

---

38. No. 1 Attack was a line-astern formation attack which gave the leader a chance to fire, followed by each succeeding fighter. No. 2 Attack enabled two fighters flying side-by-side to attack two enemy machines; it might also entail two strings of *Hurricanes* doing a co-ordinated No. 1 Attack. The No. 3 Attack was a complicated maneouvre involving three fighters simultaneously engaging a target from the rear, beam, and rear quarter. These three methods had been evolved by the RAF during the 1930's, without reference to actual combat; British aircraft had not engaged hostile fighters since the Russian campaign of 1919. Battle experience would prove these tactics to be of limited value.

39. Hitchins, *The All-Canadian Squadron*, and James J. Halley, *Royal Air Force*

Canadian authorities continued to show interest in No. 242. On December 19th the RCAF Liaison Office advised Gobeil that he was authorized to wear the new "Canada" shoulder flashes.[40] It would appear that only he, as a member of the RCAF, was considered eligible for this distinction. Other personnel asked that they, too, be allowed to put up "Canada" badges, and permission eventually was granted. Yet by the time that was allowed, some Canadians declined to wear them. According to Lorne Chambers, "All of us were ashamed of the reputation 'earned' by the 1st Canadian Army Division in busting up the English city of Aldershot.'"[41] This view was not universally shared; A.W. Taylor's recollections are that the ground crew were happy to put up "Canada" flashes.[42]

Further RCAF "official" attention was shown when Wing Commander Heakes attended the funeral of Flying Officer Coe. On February 16th the squadron was visited by representatives of the Canadian Broadcasting Corporation, intent upon doing a programme with No. 242 personnel. Again, from March 1st to 10th, Pilot Officer Hart Massey (a son of the High Commissioner) was attached to the unit in the capacity of Assistant Adjutant. Yet the RCAF connection remained sporadic; Canadian authorities did not even have complete lists of squadron members.

Early in March it appeared that the anticipated move to France might soon take place. On the 11th and 12th everyone received the mandatory "shots". The impending transfer inspired another visit by Canadian officers—this time Air Commodore G.V. Walsh and Wing Commander A.P. Campbell on the 13th. Informally the word came down from Air Marshal Saul that the move would occur about April 1st.

On March 23rd three officers from No. 13 Group Headquarters examined the squadron on scrambled interceptions, formation

Aircraft, L1000 to L9999 (Tonbridge, 1979), p. 14. Additional details of crash from recollections of Stan Turner. See also Saskatoon *Star-Phoenix*, February 3rd and March 4th, 1940.

40. Wing Commander Heakes to Squadron Leader Gobeil, December 19th, 1939. See note 15.

41. L.E. Chambers to the author, May 8th, 1980.

42. Interview with A.W. Taylor, November 22nd, 1980.

flying, air-sea firing, and tactical skills. This last item was checked by having the pilots conduct No. 1, 2, and 3 attacks on a *Blenheim*, in the turret of which sat an officer observing how closely they adhered to the book. The inspecting officers expressed great satisfaction with the squadron's performance. "A" Flight was airborne in two minutes after receiving a scramble order, and "B" Flight was off in three minutes and twenty seconds. Forthwith No. 242 was declared operational by day.[43] On March 25th "A" Flight undertook the squadron's first operational sorties—convoy patrols by Flight Lieutenant Miller, Flying Officer Chambers, and Pilot Officers Brown, McKnight, MacQueen, and Wiens. Over the next four days the two flights alternated on these duties while the pilots practiced night flying (two hours per man). At last the squadron was declared ready for overseas service (meaning France) and personnel were sent on leave preparatory to departure on April 8th.

While these steps were being taken, Fighter Command ordered that two officers should proceed to Lille-Seclin, in France, to survey the facilities being used by No. 85 Squadron, the unit No. 242 was to replace. Accordingly, on April 4th, Flying Officer MacDonald (the Adjutant) and Pilot Officer Stansfeld went to Hendon. From there they flew to France on the 6th. Two days later MacDonald was back at Church Fenton with a detachment of airmen from No. 85 Squadron. On the 9th Flight Lieutenants Miller and Sullivan, accompanied by six airmen, proceeded to France for further liaison with No. 85 Squadron. General movement orders reached No. 242 on April 10th; the unit was to travel by air, rail, and sea to the Continent between the 14th and 21st.

These orders were obsolete even as they were being transmitted. On April 8th the Germans had invaded Denmark, and on the 9th they descended upon Norway. The "phoney war" was over. As the situation deteriorated, higher authority cancelled any movements which might disrupt anticipated operations. No. 242 Squad-

43. Not all records or recollections of these tests are in agreement; they may have been carried out over a two-day period, rather than one as suggested by the unit ORB. Howitt's logbook mentions no flying on the 23rd but lists 55 minutes of "test exercises" on the 22nd. Stansfeld's logbook has entries for March 23rd ("Firing at Catfoss range", "Group test-formation") and 24th ("Squadron test formation"). Miller's logbook has similar entries for the 23rd and 24th. The *Blenheim* is mentioned in no document, but is recalled by Turner and Stansfeld independently.

ron's transfer was reversed on the 12th. The advance party of three officers and six airmen was recalled; the men were back at Church Fenton by April 17th, the pilots having flown some half-dozen or more uneventful sorties during their sojourn in France.

The unit resumed night flying training and convoy patrols, operating from their dispersal sites. Such work was not without strain, incident, or tragedy. On April 18th an airman was killed accidentally while a *Hurricane's* guns were being test-fired. Another airman died after being struck by a rotating propeller on the night of May 6th. That same evening Pilot Officer Howitt recorded in his diary that he had spent two hours and fifteen minutes on night flying, which had left him very fatigued. Nevertheless, by the end of May 11th the squadron had been declared operational for night duties.

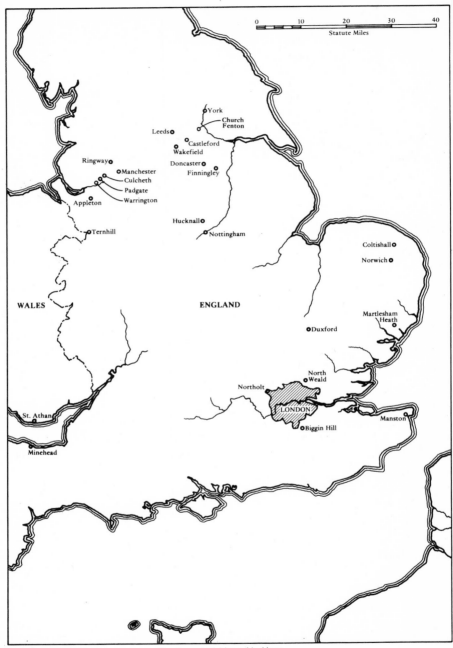

Statute Miles

York
Church Fenton
Leeds
Castleford
Wakefield
Ringway
Manchester
Culcheth
Doncaster
Finningley
Padgate
Appleton
Warrington
Ternhill
Hucknall
Nottingham
Coltishall
Norwich
WALES
ENGLAND
Martlesham Heath
Duxford
North Weald
Northolt
LONDON
Manston
St. Athan
Biggin Hill
Minehead

Map 1 - **Activities and incidents**
November 1939 - May 1940

Detached Operations in France

At dawn on May 10th, 1940 the great German offensive began, with blows falling simultaneously on Holland, Belgium, Luxembourg, and France. From the outset the RAF took heavy casualties in the severe fighting.

For No. 242 Squadron everything was in flux. On the morning of the 13th they received word that they were to go to France. That order was cancelled. Instead, No. 13 Group Headquarters instructed that four pilots be sent to Manston for duty. Flight Lieutenant Sullivan, accompanied by Pilot Officers Grassick, McKnight, and Turner, left at 6:00 that evening. The following day they proceeded to the Continent, to be attached to RAF units already in action.

On the 15th "A" Flight was called upon for overseas duty, only to have the order reversed the same day. It was re-issued on the 16th; Flight Lieutenant Miller, Flying Officer Chambers, and Pilot Officers Brown, Deacon, MacQueen, and Wiens left at once for France. No. 242 Squadron's initiation to battle therefore was not as a unit, but through these two groups of pilots. All ten, though devoid of combat experience, now flew with *Hurricane* squadrons committed to a fierce battle.

The records of Nos. 607 and 615 Squadrons, to which the first four pilots were attached, are extremely vague, many documents having been lost in the subsequent hasty departure from France. Even so, much can be learned from the logbooks of McKnight and Grassick, which have been preserved in Britain and Canada. The Grassick logbook, however, is curiously inaccurate as to dates, as though its owner had not maintained it for several days, then had rushed to make the necessary entries.[1]

The four men flew to Vitry-en-Artois on May 14th and were immediately thrust into action. In the course of a patrol that morning by No. 607, apparently in company with another squadron, twenty-four *Hurricanes* met fifteen *Hs126* army co-operation aircraft and forty-five escorting *Bf109's* near Louvain. At least ten of the enemy were shot down, but so were four *Hurricanes*, including the one flown by Sullivan. He became the first member of No. 242 Squadron to die in action. A report reaching the unit suggested that he had been fired on while descending by parachute.[2]

McKnight flew two patrols on his first day in France, over Louvain (where he became involved in the air battle) and then over Zeebrugge. On the 15th he flew a sortie in the Lille-Cambrai sector, and another in the Lille-Arras area on the 16th. McKnight and Grassick were then transferred to No. 615 Squadron, operating from Moorselle, Belgium. They joined their new unit at once, and made several flights before nightfall.

On May 17th McKnight flew a two-hour reconnaissance along

1. McKnight's logbook is held by the Public Records Office in Great Britain (PRO Reference AIR 4, Document 77). The Grassick logbook was loaned to this writer by Mrs. Una Grassick. Turner's logbook for this period was lost during later operations; the fate of Sullivan's logbook is unknown.

2. Hitchins, in *The All-Canadian Squadron*, mentions only that four *Hurricanes* and ten enemy aircraft were destroyed, noting the loss of Sullivan and the report of his being shot at while parachuting. Secondary sources have supplied the types and numbers of enemy machines and the fact that twenty-four *Hurricanes* were involved. See Calgary *Herald*, October 2, 1940; Sir Harry Brittain, *Come the Three Corners*; (London, 1940), p. 85; Peter J. Field, *Canada's Wings* (London, 1942), p. 35. All seem to draw on a common, unidentified "official" document which the author has been unable to trace. Field suggests that all four were on this patrol. Grassick and McKnight almost certainly were, but Turner has no personal recollection of the action. He has mentioned a report that Sullivan was caught in a crossfire from two *Hs126's*.

the Arras-Cambrai road. Later that day he participated in an offensive patrol near Cambrai. They were stooging around that city when, at 7:40 p.m., seven *Bf109's* attacked the *Hurricanes* from 10,000 feet. They were followed by eight more. McKnight radioed a warning to his fellows, climbed steeply to the left, and came up behind a Messerschmitt. From 250 yards he opened fire, and smoke began issuing from the *'109*. In all he fired four short bursts, and the enemy machine crashed.[3]

McKnight flew one patrol on the 18th and two on the 19th, including one sortie over Douai (when his fuel tanks were holed by small arms fire) and a strafing trip down the Arras-Cambrai road. Later on the 19th he returned to England, flying from Norrent Fontes to Kenley, probably in the company of Turner and Grassick who also reached England that day. Word was despatched to them that they were granted seven days' leave. This was formally cancelled within twenty-four hours when it became apparent that their services would be needed for further important operations. Word of the cancellation evidently failed to reach the trio, for they do not re-appear in squadron records until the 26th.[4]

The experiences of "Slim" Grassick in France had been fully as exciting as McKnight's, but his logbook is the only terse account of his activities; no Combat Reports have been traced to describe his several engagements. Grassick's entries are given below in full, but as mentioned earlier the dates are suspect and should be altered by one day.[5] But let the logbook speak, however awkwardly, of his days in northern France and Belgium:

3. The date of this action is something of a puzzle; a Combat Report submitted by McKnight is dated May 19th, but his logbook gives the date as May 17th. The author, weighing probabilities, accepts the earlier date and thus admits to an error in his earlier book, *The Tumbling Sky* (Canada's Wings, Stittsville, 1978).

4. See Chapter 3, note 1.

5. Grassick gives May 12th as the day he flew to Manston, while No. 242's documents, McKnight's logbook, and Howitt's diary all agree that it was May 13th. The quartet must therefore have flown to France on the 14th—not the 13th as given by Grassick. Assuming that all his entries for this period are out by some degree, the move to Moorselle would have been on May 16th (as entered by McKnight) rather than the 15th (as given by Grassick).

May 12—Church Fenton to Manston—2.00 [two hours]—
    Posted as reinforcements to France with F/L
    Sullivan, P/O Turner, P/O McKnight.

May 13—Manston to Vitry—1.45

May 13—Patrol east of Brussels—1.20—Went with 607
    Squadron—Contacted ME.109

May 14—Patrol Louvaine—1.30

May 14—Vitry to Abbeville—.45—Joined 615 Sqdn. Changed
    letters to KNX on a/c [He had flown out on LE-B.]

May 14—Patrol Brussels—2.00—Got a ME.109. Landed at
    Vitry.

May 14—Patrol west of Brussels—2.30

May 15—Vitry offensive—.20—Ju.88 confirmed

May 15—Vitry-Moorselle—.45

May 15—Patrol Brussels—2.00—ME.109 confirmed.

May 16—Patrol Arras—2.00

May 16—Patrol Arras-Cambrai Road—2.30

May 16—Offensive Patrol—1.30—Shooting up Troops

May 17—Dawn Patrol, Cambrai—1.30

May 18—Moorselle-Norrent Fontes—1.45

May 18—Patrol Arras-Lille-Ghent—1.00

May 18—Norrent Fontes-Kenley—2.00

May 19—Kenley-Croydon—.20

May 20—Croydon-Hatfield—1.00

May 21—Kenley-Lille-Manston—2.00—Took documents to
    British troops at Lille aerodrome with T. Eryes.

"A" Flight had meanwhile proceeded to France on May 16th.
Its departure had been the occasion of a wryly humorous incident
later recalled by Lorne Chambers:

The first section and the flight was led by Flight Lieutenant
Don Miller, and I was leading the second section. After we
had gone about 50 miles from our base at Church Fenton in
Yorkshire, I could hear the Operations Control Officer
calling our leader, but there was no response from him. I
looked over at him and it was obvious that he had heard
them but had no intention of answering in case they were
going to recall us. They then called me, and I also did not
respond. Then one of the pilots (no name mentioned) called
us on the radio and in normal military "correct" jargon said,

"Hey you guys—wake up—base is calling you." This of course let the "cat out of the bag" and we could no longer pretend to be beyond radio range, so Don responded. Much to our relief the Controller only wanted to wish us luck.[6]

They joined No. 85 Squadron at Lille/Seclin and enjoyed a good night's rest.[7] The following day they were operational. Flying Officer Deacon flew three patrols over the aerodrome logging almost one hour and forty minutes. The others undoubtedly were on duty as well, but no details have come to light.[8]

On Saturday, May 18th, Miller flew one sortie, a dawn patrol over Forêt de Mormal lasting an hour. Deacon, who had gone to bed at 11:00 p.m. the night before, was up at 3:00 a.m. and flew four patrols that day, all apparently without incident. Elsewhere disaster struck. In the course of a patrol (variously described as an early morning interception or as an offensive patrol in the Le Cateau quadrant) Brown, Chambers, and Wiens were shot down. In a letter home, Wiens would describe his own experiences, illustrating the terrible conditions under which RAF squadrons were fighting:

> I am at present in a hospital in England, and have been here for the past two weeks. Previous to that I completed an extensive tour of northern France which took in Lille, Valenciennes, Cambrai, St. Pol, Le Touquet, Etaples, Boulogne, and then home. [Wiens appears to refer both to places from which he flew and through which he was evacuated.] I was shot down by a Messerschmitt 110 or rather by about four of them. We were out on patrol and ran into about twelve of them and did we have a scrap!
>
> The war in the air today makes shows like Dawn Patrol look like Sunday School. It wasn't my first scrap but previous to that we never had such odds against us.

6. L.E. Chambers to the author, letter dated May 8th, 1980.

7. No. 85 Squadron's ORB gives their reporting date as May 14th; this is clearly in error.

8. Details of Miller's flying taken from his logbook, loaned to the author. Deacon's adventures are set out in "Supplement to 242 Squadron's Previous Advance Combat Report", a resumé of his experiences and dated May 22nd, 1940. The original was sent from No. 13 Group to Headquarters of Fighter Command; a copy was kindly provided by the RAF Museum, Hendon.

We saw them first and went right in on their tail. I got one with my first burst and then followed a general melee. I was trying to maneouvre for another one when a 110 nearly collided with me. The rear gunner and I had an argument, however. I gave him about 500 rounds and could see him fold up. I don't know whether the plane crashed or not, but if it did I have three.[9]

My engine cracked up owing to bullets in the cooling and oil system. I did not parachute because it isn't safe anymore owing to parachute troops. The French pot them on the way down.

I crashed in a valley on top of some trees. I immediately wrote the plane off but got away with a bit of concussion and a stiff leg and a cut face. I was out for an hour or so and it is lucky she did not burn. . . . The French found me first and thought I was a German. Three of them pulled guns on me and I thought I was done but I passed out again and woke up in British hands, so it was oke. I went from one hospital to another in this retreat. They were all bombed so you may well believe I am glad to be back.[10]

Brown had been wounded in the right leg when he was downed; one report suggested he had been hit by five bullets in both legs. He was taken to the same aid station as Wiens. They were put into an ambulance heading for Cambrai, where they were to be hospitalized. When their driver learned that the city had been captured he headed for the coast, and in due course both pilots were evacuated to England. Chambers was less fortunate. His aircraft had exploded and he had bailed out of the flaming wreck, suffering burns to his face, hands, right leg, and both feet. He arrived at the aid post fifteen minutes after his companions had left. He, too, was put in a vehicle bound for Cambrai:

When my ambulance driver found that Cambrai had fallen

9. This statement is rather odd in that Wiens mentions firing upon two aircraft only. Since this was not his first action, it is possible that he claimed an enemy machine on the 17th.

10. Letter to his brother (unnamed), republished in Saskatoon *Star-Pheonix*, July 4th, 1940. Wiens did not return to No. 242. Late in 1940 he was posted to Canada for service as an instructor. On May 21st, 1941 he lost his life by staying at the controls of a burning *Anson* while three others bailed out.

he took me to another hospital 9 km. away, left me there, and he took off for the coast. The next day the Germans overran the hospital and I was a prisoner.[11]

The 19th proved to be the most hectic day of all as the Germans advanced relentlessly; by late afternoon they would be in Douai, forcing No. 85 Squadron to fall back to Merville after destroying documents and abandoning kit. Flight Lieutenant Miller flew three patrols that day, beginning with an offensive sortie over Valenciennes, Le Cateau, and Cambrai lasting two hours and ten minutes. The second trip was a 45 minute standing patrol over the Lille air base. Several *Bf109's* appeared and Miller's *Hurricane* was badly shot about in the port wing. Before repairs could be effected the airfield was bombed by approximately eighteen *He111's*; he was scrambled in his damaged airplane to pursue the enemy, though without any luck.

Pilot Officer Deacon, who had caught less than two hours' sleep the previous night, flew four sorties on May 19th. The second one was just after noon, when the *He111's* were bombing the airfield; he was scrambled with several other fighters. Deacon saw two Heinkels descending in flames; he followed the second one down to ensure that it was not going to escape, then climbed to engage the main formation.

He attacked an *He111* from above and behind on the starboard quarter, firing three bursts that used up most of his ammunition. A German gunner took a few shots at him, but the bullets went wide and Deacon's machine guns silenced the enemy. The Heinkel pilot throttled back. Deacon had no time to break away; instead he roared directly over the bomber, looking into the cockpit as he went by. The bomber's starboard engine was burning and the pilot bailed out. Deacon's *Hurricane* was unscathed. He turned to engage the *He111* again but saw another *Hurricane* following it down. It would need no further attention.[12]

Deacon's third patrol of the day lasted 75 minutes. He was so exhausted that he fell asleep in his cockpit three times while over

11. See note 6. Curiously, Chambers was not formally reported to be in German hands until July 24th, 1940. His first letter home after capture would be the classic plea of prisoners-of-war for cigarettes and chocolate. See *Vancouver Sun*, July 25th and October 17th, 1940.

12. See note 8. No Combat Report for this action was ever filed.

enemy territory! Following another sortie, with No. 85 preparing to abandon Lille aerodrome, the three Canadians from No. 242 took off with different orders—to fly back to Church Fenton by way of Manston, a trip that required two hours and fifty minutes air time. On the way out from Lille, Miller's *Hurricane* was hit by groundfire that holed his oil tank; it was a near-miracle that he got back across the Channel without his engine seizing.

Pilot Officer MacQueen had written to his father on May 15th, on the eve of his departure for France, and again on May 21st, just after he returned with Miller and Deacon to England. Through digests of these letters, published in Canadian newspapers, we learn some of his adventures during the brief French tour, although specific dates and places are not mentioned;

> On one occasion he was forced down when his engine stalled and while he endeavoured to fix it he was machine-gunned by German fliers. He crawled under the plane until the attackers withdrew, and managed to escape uninjured and take off in his plane again. On another occasion he was forced down to land, somewhere in France, and had an embarrassing time trying to convince a mob of angry peasants that he was not a German flier. Fortunately, he said, his high school French pulled him through. . . .
>
> He said that during the six days he hardly had time to eat, never washed and never took his clothes off. "Sleep was an hour here and there", he said. During this time he also was engaged twice with German fighters, but managed to get away.[13]

Miller, MacQueen, and Deacon had witnessed terrible scenes. In his report, Deacon mentioned a Sergeant Pilot in No. 85 Squadron who had shot down a *Bf109*, then saw a bomber apparently firing 20-mm shells at him. The Sergeant shot it down, only to discover that it had been a *Blenheim* firing two red cartridges, the identifying colours of the day. In the heat of battle it was hard to avoid tragic mistakes. The three Canadians were given seven days leave on their return to Church Fenton; it was cancelled before they could use it.

---

13. "Another City Pilot Missing", Calgary *Herald*, June 12th, 1940. The statement concerning "six days" is questionable; if MacQueen returned on the 19th he would have been on the Continent only four days.

The story of "A" Flight would be incomplete without recounting the adventures of some of the ground personnel. Several tradesmen had been flown to the Continent on the 16th in a *Ju52* commandeered from SABENA, the Belgian airline. Their ranks included at least eight Canadians—Leading Aircraftmen A.W. Taylor (Victoria), A.M. Martin (Edmonton), E.T. Einboden (Lancing, Ontario), and T.L. Galbraith (Winnipeg), plus Aircraftmen First Class E.T. Cameron (Port Hood, Nova Scotia), C.T. Gibbons (Nanaimo), D.R. Stephens (Duncan, British Columbia), and G.W. Sleigh (Vancouver). Taylor and Martin subsequently wrote letters describing their experiences and these epistles were published in hometown papers. Their detailed accounts, scarcely touched by censors, may have made amusing, even exciting reading at home, but they actually show a dreadful picture of a military organization ill-prepared to feed, shelter, or protect them. Taylor, whose working knowledge of French was a particular asset, wrote a letter that combined personal observation with rumour:

We left England by a big army transport plane, landing at our destination without incident and immediately found billets in a French farmyard. My French came in handy when we learned the farmer had run out of rations. I and some pals went scouting for food and made householders understand that we were hungry. We had some swell meals for a few francs.

After a short time we got orders to pack a few things together and make ready for leaving. The bombs were falling. I was detailed to take a party and help clear the "institute" [auxiliary stores section operated by the Navy, Army, and Air Force Institute, better known as NAAFI]. After packing all we could, we were told by the "institute" manager to help ourselves. We had a great feed of tinned fruit etc and I took my overcoat out of my lower pack and filled the pack with cartons of cigarettes. I had several thousands of them.

Finally we left the place and headed for another destination, Merville, where the groundcrew were briefly accommodated in an abandoned farmhouse, complete with luxurious feather beds. There we were bombed again, but nobody seemed to mind it. What made me feel bad was the stream of refugees, mile after mile of them, old people and young children, and all looking so helpless. I gave away box after box of chocolates to them. The "institute" fellows objected a bit, but we soon shut them up.

Then we learned that we had just left our "drome" in time as the "Germs" sent droves of kites over and blew the deuce out of the railroad station, thinking we were moving by rail.

All this time our boys were bringing Gerry kites down like flies. We shot down six to their one, on an average. The pilots usually baled out in their chutes. This baling out is the only snag there is, there being so many German para- chutists now, the people on the ground are more than likely to shoot first and ask questions afterwards. One of our pilots baled out of a "blazer" and the Belgians machine-gunned him as he came down and killed him.

Arriving at our second destination we had a few hours peace, but only a few for Gerry bombed us again. With all this bombing we had no casualties. So we moved down to Boulogne where we were quartered in a rest camp. That night we were bombed again. The next morning we boarded a ship for Dover. Arriving there we took train to ——. [Lon- don and Biggin Hill]

But I want to go back to France again. After seeing how it is there, I feel that I cannot do enough. I really amazed myself, as even during the heavy bombardment and aerial battles, when others were in shelters, I and three more Cana- dians stayed out in the open and started the aircraft. Then we would take cover. Strange that I felt no fear whatever, and it gives me lots of confidence for the tough times to come.[14]

Taylor's letter, explicit as it was, did not tell the full story. Ted Einboden had been one of the Canadians helping him to start *Hurricanes* under fire. At Boulogne the airmen had been confined to a Nissen hut pending evacuation, and this had been very trying on the nerves of most during bombing raids. Taylor, with confidence in the hut's ability to endure a near miss, and certain of instant death should it sustain a direct hit, put on his steel helmet and went to sleep. Four years were to pass before he would confront death directly and learn the meaning of gut-wrenching fear.[15]

14. "Were Bombed Every Night", Victoria *Colonist*, June 20th, 1940.

15. Interview with A.W. Taylor, November 23rd, 1980.

Archibald Martin's letter home, summarized in the Edmonton *Journal*, was less detailed but equally vibrant. It mentioned his flight from England to Arras, which was bombed minutes after their arrival. From there they went to Lille (home of No. 85 Squadron) where he saw some lorries bombed and blown to smithereens. That night the house in which he and several others were billeted was bombed. The building collapsed around them, but Martin escaped injury. The next day he and a comrade were strafed by a German fighter; they sought shelter behind a brick wall. Soon afterwards they were sent to Boulogne from whence they were evacuated by boat; the port itself fell to the Germans on May 24th.[16]

No. 242's personnel had thus received their baptism of fire. The pilots had shot down roughly half-a-dozen enemy aircraft (claimed by Deacon, Grassick, McKnight, and Wiens) and had suffered four casualties (Sullivan killed, Chambers a POW, Brown and Wiens wounded). They had witnessed the debacle in the making, and yet they had been fortunate. Like the other RAF squadrons in France, they at least had been operating from within a secure British perimeter. On their next visit to France they would encounter chaos that mounted by the day.

16. "City Flier Escapes Death as Nazi Bombs Fall Nearby", Edmonton *Journal*, June 25th, 1940.

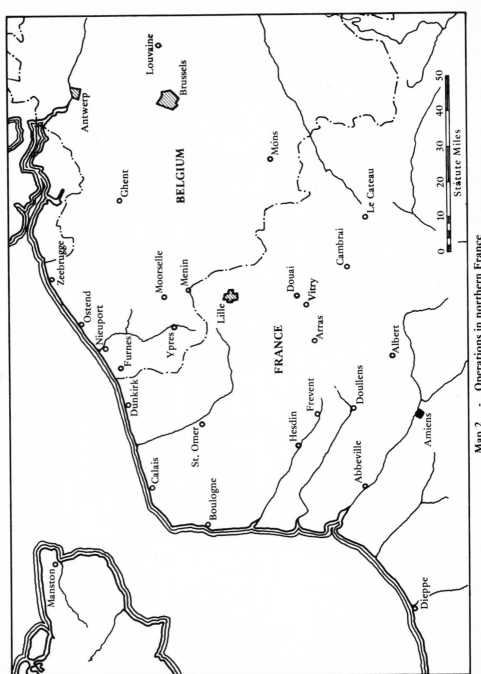

Map 2 - Operations in northern France
May June 1940

Operations from Britain

While some of No. 242 Squadron's personnel had been engaged in France, Squadron Leader Gobeil and eleven other pilots had stood by, ready for night operations from Church Fenton. At noon on May 21st they received orders from No. 13 Group Headquarters to proceed to Biggin Hill. A detachment of mechanics was despatched immediately, followed by twelve *Hurricanes*. These took off at 7:00 p.m. and encountered the London balloon barrage on the way to their destination. The surviving pilots of "A" Flight reported back to the squadron at about this time. Those groundcrew who had gone with them to France returned on or near the 26th, together with Grassick, McKnight, and Turner.[1] As the veterans of the French adventure trickled back, a new phase of operations began to unfold.

1. According to his logbook, McKnight rejoined the squadron on May 26th. Grassick's logbook constitutes less direct evidence; he simply recorded no flying from May 22nd to May 26th, then logged a patrol on the 27th. The matter of the date is important, for in *Aces High* Chris Shores, without citing sources, credits Turner with two confirmed victories and one "probable" on May 25th. These claims are not recorded in *The All Canadian Squadron*, nor can Combat Reports for the purported actions be traced.

At the outset of the Battle of France there had been six RAF fighter squadrons on the Continent. Four more had been despatched immediately to support them. On May 13th Fighter Command had sent 32 pilots and machines—the equivalent of two further squadrons--as additional reinforcements; this was the move that had taken Grassick, McKnight, Sullivan, and Turner to France and Belgium. Responding to further appeals for fighters, Air Ministry had then ordered eight flights—including No. 242's "A" Flight—to France on May 16th, a move that Air Chief Marshal Sir Hugh Dowding (Air Officer Commanding in Chief, Fighter Command) had regarded with misgiving. Dowding subsequently recounted the thought processes on the part of the Air Ministry that had led to the action:

> This was done under the impression that the loss of 8 Half Squadrons would affect me less than that of 4 entire Squadrons, because it was supposed that I should be able to rebuild on the nuclei left behind. But this assumption was incorrect because I had neither the time nor the personnel available for purposes of reconstruction.[2]

By May 20th most of the RAF's squadrons had been withdrawn from France, having suffered great losses and been forced from their bases by the enemy advance. Notwithstanding these developments, the French Premier, Paul Renaud, had urged his British ally to despatch ten more fighter squadrons to the Continent. This move was vigorously opposed by Dowding, who recognized that the Battle of France was already lost. On May 15th he had met with the British Cabinet and had put the facts to them bluntly—France was a bottomless pit, which could absorb British pilots and aircraft without any effect. Better, he argued, that the fighters be retained in England for the defence of the homeland.

Prime Minister Churchill accepted these facts reluctantly; during a visit to Paris he ignored previous advice and cabled for the transfer of six fighter squadrons to the Continent. In the end, Dowding's views were sustained. As a compromise with their consciences the British allowed fighter squadrons in England to patrol over French territory. This was an empty gesture, however, until

2. *The Battle of Britain*, Air Chief Marshal Dowding's despatch of August 20th, 1941 to the Secretary of State for Air, printed as a Supplement to the *London Gazette*, September 11th, 1946.

the patrols coincided with an operation that came under their umbrella—*Dynamo*, better known as the Dunkirk evacuation.[3]

It was in keeping with these programmes of "limited support" that No. 242 had been committed in penny packets to the Battle of France, and now undertook patrols over the French coast. On the afternoon of May 22nd eight of the unit's *Hurricanes* took off to patrol a triangle bounded roughly by Arras, Albert, and Frevent. In his diary Pilot Officer Howitt noted that they had seen a ship burning in the Channel, and that accurate flak was encountered. Between Doullens and Hesdin the pilots, led by Flight Lieutenant Miller, spotted a group of *Hs 126* reconnaissance machines at 4,000 feet.

The first victim fell to Pilot Officers Stansfeld and MacQueen, whose two Combat Reports complement each other so perfectly that they merit quoting in entirety. Stansfeld wrote:

I sighted enemy aircraft approaching cloud. I opened fire from the rear which apparently silenced rear gunner. P/O MacQueen then opened fire on my left. The enemy aircraft stalled and headed for the ground, nose down. It crashed and burst into flames.

MacQueen's part was a bit more complicated, apparently because he did not have the element of surprise when he engaged the *Hs 126* a minute or two later. His Combat Report read:

P/O Stansfeld first delivered attack. Believe he silenced rear gun. Enemy aircraft climbed up to protection of small clouds. I climbed to an advantage above him and attacked him—while he was outlined in cloud. His machine stalled and fell towards the ground. I pulled out of my dive and saw him headed towards the ground. P/O Stansfeld saw him crash—thus confirming my victory.

Flying Officer Graafstra and Pilot Officer Madore spotted an *Hs 126* flying at 50 feet. Each man carried out five beam and quarter attacks, forcing the enemy machine to land in a field. The crew took to some bushes while the *Hurricanes* made one strafing pass

3. See Francis K. Mason, *Battle Over Britain* (London, 1969), pp. 114-115; L.F. Ellis, *The War in France and Flanders, 1939-40* (London, 1953), pp. 57-58, 60-61.

after another. Finally, their ammunition exhausted, the two men headed for home, uncertain as to whether they might claim their target as "destroyed".

While these engagements were raging, Flight Lieutenant Miller was patrolling 3,000 feet above the main action. Noting an *Hs 126* that was attempting to escape into clouds, he attacked from above and behind, pouring bullets into his quarry until it burst into flames. The crash of the Henschel was witnessed by Squadron Leader E.V. Knowles, the Commanding Officer of No. 56 Squadron, which had also participated in the massacre of the *Hs 126's*.[4]

No. 242 was now well and truly launched upon its operational career. As the war intensified, some pilots reacted by looking inward. According to James Howitt, this was the case with G.A. Madore, who talked of going to church more often, realizing that "there just might be more to life than flying and drinking". If Madore was serious about these things, he would have virtually no time to act upon such introspection.

On May 23rd a flight of No. 242 Squadron and one from No. 32 Squadron escorted a reconnaissance *Blenheim* over northern France (7:30-10:30 a.m.), apparently refuelling at Manston before proceeding over the Continent.[5] Near Ypres the Canadians were attacked by some eighteen *Bf 109's* while a dozen more took No. 32 from the rear. Pilot Officer Benzie was wounded but managed to parachute to safety; he was duly evacuated to England *via* Dunkirk. Flying Officer Graafstra and Pilot Officer Madore were shot down and killed. Pilot Officer Smiley was also hit, but he baled out of his burning *Hurricane* and was taken prisoner.[6] He was sent to a German

---

4. No. 242 Squadron's Form 540 gives the time of this flight as 1:30-4:30 p.m., but the Combat Reports submitted give the time of the fighting itself as 4:25-4:38 p.m.—another indication of the unit diary's unreliability. In this case Combat Reports filed by personnel of No. 56 Squadron agree with those of No. 242's pilots as to the time of the action.

5. Hitchins, *The All Canadian Squadron*, mentions that this flight took place between 12:45 and 2:15 p.m., with an uneventful patrol being conducted in the early morning. In the cards he compiled on CAN/RAF personnel he gives the time as stated in this narrative.

6. The four *Hurricanes* lost were P2550 (Benzie), P2730 (Madore), P2809 (Graafstra), and P3392 (Smiley). James J. Halley, *Royal Air Force Aircraft, P1000 to P9999* (Tonbridge, 1978).

base hospital for an operation to remove shell fragments from his head. As he regained consciousness, Smiley discovered a friend in the next bed—Lorne Chambers, who had been shot down five days before.[7]

Later that day Squadron Leader Gobeil led Red Section on a "survey" some 20 miles inland from Boulogne. Flying at 6,000 feet amid heavy cloud, he lost his bearings and turned back toward the coast. As the section broke cloud near Berck and circled to determine their position, Gobeil saw a light blue *Bf 109E* at 2,500 feet; the time was 2:45 p.m. He dived alone on the enemy machine, snapped off a good burst, then overshot. As he circled for another pass he was subjected to intense flak and a shell burst close to his *Hurricane*. Gobeil climbed to rejoin his comrades, none of whom had witnessed his combat. It was an inconclusive action, but it marked the first time that a member of the RCAF had engaged an enemy aircraft.

The next morning, the 24th, No. 242 flew two patrols over the French coast, the first at 5:00 a.m. and the second at 11:00 a.m. The latter was conducted over the Dunkirk-St. Omer-Boulogne area. During the course of this patrol two *Hurricanes* were lost, killing Pilot Officers R.L. Hill (P3266) and J.W. Mitchell (P3272).

No. 242's Squadron's records fail to give a satisfactory account of this tragedy. The unit diary recorded that the fighters encountered intense anti-aircraft fire which brought down the two machines. This version is supported by W.A. Waterton, who has stated that he saw gun flashes below at the time. However, he no longer has his logbook to refresh his memory.

This story is contradicted by the independent recollections of three pilots—James Howitt, Arthur Deacon, and Noel Stansfeld—all of whom agree that Hill and Mitchell were lost through a mid-air collision over the sea with no flak about. Stansfeld recorded the collision in his logbook while Howitt mentioned it in his diary; in April 1980 the latter vividly remembered staring at the accident goggle-eyed. "Nobody said a word. We just watched them go down." Deacon, flying in a section behind theirs, observed one *Hurricane* chew the tailplane off the other, then saw the two aircraft start

7. "Vernon Pilot, Prisoner, Meets Pal in Hospital Ward", Vancouver *Sun*, October 17th, 1940.

their final plunge. They had probably been the No. 2 and No. 3 men in a three-plane vee-formation, weaving and on the lookout for enemy aircraft when the accident occurred.[8]

Again on the 25th No. 242 carried out patrols over France, flying from Manston, where a squadron detachment of one NCO and eight airmen re-armed and refuelled the eight *Hurricanes*. In the morning they flew an uneventful beat over Calais, Lille, and Dunkirk, although Howitt returned early with his engine overheating. That afternoon they set out to prowl about Ypres and Lille. Later, in the context of a formal Combat Report, Squadron Leader Gobeil described what happened:

> We were flying at about 23,000 feet just below cloud into which we would climb and descend occasionally. At about 14.30 hours I noticed a ME 110 by itself ease out of the clouds to our left and go back in. I immediately called up the section on the R/T and turned to the right to get into the sun. We were then about 8-10 miles N.W. of Courtrai.
>
> The E.A. dropped out of the clouds and began a medium dive down. I let him go down some distance and then took after him. I think he must have seen me then, as he steepened his dive and began to turn towards me to the right. I had no difficulty in overtaking him, however, so he may not have seen me.
>
> I came in on him from the right quarter astern until he completely filled the sight, when I allowed full left deflection and opened fire. I got in about a 5 second burst when I did a quick left hand turn and levelled out. I saw the machine continue down from the attack with greyish black vapour coming out of the right motor. The E.A. continued to the ground where it crash landed in a field. I did not follow it down as we were on the last leg of our patrol and were only 3 a/c. P/O Stansfeld my No. 2 saw the E.A. come down in the field.
>
> I circled until my two wing men joined me—P/O MacQueen told me he had spotted 12 ME 109s about 10,000

8. Interview with Howitt, April 29th, 1980; letters from A.H. Deacon to the author, dated April 13th and May 6th, 1980; Stansfeld logbook and interview, November 20th, 1980; telephone conversation with W.A. Waterton, October 19th, 1980.

feet above us when he signalled to go home. We had been on patrol for about 1 hr. 45 mins.

Gobeil had fired some 800 rounds and was credited with one *Bf 110* destroyed—the first enemy aircraft shot down by a member of the RCAF.

May 25th saw No. 242 suffer another casualty. Pilot Officer Waterton force-landed in England and sustained head injuries that rendered him non-operational. The circumstances of his crash again reflect the state of No. 242's records and the unreliability of distant memories. The unit ORB mentioned engine trouble. In a letter to his parents Waterton wrote that he had been hit by flak over the French coast, momentarily lost control, and crashed in England, waking up in hospital with no recollection of how he had gotten down.[9] Yet as of October 1980 he was uncertain as to whether he had actually been hit by anti-aircraft fire or had suffered oxygen failure. Noel Stansfeld's logbook noted that Waterton had sustained a memory loss on the 25th, without stating the cause.

On May 26th No. 242 contributed only three sorties; Pilot Officers Deacon, Howitt, and Jones were involved in escorting eight *Blenheims* from Hawkinge to Menin in Belgium and back to Manston. No enemy fighters were encountered, but Howitt recorded in his diary that they had faced heavy flak. The unit was ordered to stand down for the balance of the day. During these hours the squadron achieved something resembling full strength again as Turner, Grassick, and McKnight, who had earlier been despatched to France, rejoined No. 242 while it rested at Biggin Hill. Yet the casualties of the last few days had left the squadron stretched; at dawn of the 27th they still had only twelve pilots. That was the day that Operation *Dynamo*—the wholesale removal of a British army and over 123,000 French soldiers—got underway at Dunkirk.

Although some non-essential personnel had been evacuated during the previous few days, with a systematic withdrawal from Boulogne taking place on May 23rd, *Dynamo* was not initiated until the evening of May 26th. At the time it seemed a desperate, forlorn gamble which might perhaps rescue 45,000 troops. Even on the 27th—the first full day of evacuations—only 5,718 troops were landed in Britain, and on the 28th the figure was just 18,527. Thanks

9. "Albertan Survives Wreck After Plane Hit", Edmonton *Journal*, July 18th, 1940.

to German indecision and its own skilful rearguard actions, however, the British Expeditionary Force was granted more than a week to extricate itself from the Continent.

Fighter Command aided the Dunkirk evacuation as much as its limited resources would permit. As of the 27th some twenty squadrons were committed to covering the ships and loading facilities of the port. From the beginning they were severely strained. The RAF had to make a choice—whether to fly many small patrols, giving thin but relatively continuous cover, or to carry out limited numbers of big patrols, meaning strong cover at times and almost no protection at intervals. The former method was employed at first, but it was soon abandoned in favour of the latter. Unfortunately, several *Luftwaffe* raids developed in the absence of *Hurricanes* and *Spitfires*, thus giving rise to Army accusations of having been abandoned. Even when fighter cover was provided, it was not always seen to be present, for air battles frequently raged on the flanks of the Dunkirk area, rather than over the port itself. The brunt of the fighting fell on No. 11 Group, which compiled the following statistics of its efforts:[10]

Date	Patrols	Daily Flying Hours	E/A Destroyed
May 27th	23	536	38
May 28th	11	576	23
May 29th	9	674	65
May 30th	9	704	—
May 31st	8	490	38
June 1st	8	558	43
June 2nd	4	231	35
June 3rd	4	339	—
June 4th	3	234	—

No. 242 Squadron figured prominently in this epic evacuation. Each morning the remnants of the unit would fly to Manston, conduct two or three patrols, and return to Biggin Hill in the evening. Their task was simple yet crucial—to cover the area between Furnes and Dunkirk, beating off any German aircraft that might come near the British Expeditionary Force and those French units that were

10. *The Evacuation of the Allied Armies From Dunkirk and Neighbouring Beaches*, Vice-Admiral Sir Bertram H. Ramsay's despatch of June 18th, 1940 to the Lords Commissioners of the Admiralty, printed as a Supplement to the *London Gazette*, July 17th, 1947. As will be seen, the figures for enemy aircraft destroyed were overly optimistic.

being hurried out of the shrinking coastal pocket. Nobody sat down to describe "the big picture" to the pilots. It was not necessary. The heroic panorama was spread out below them. Knowing the battle's importance, they gave their all daily.

Although RAF fighters tangled frequently with the enemy on May 27th, losing fourteen aircraft in the process, No. 242's sorties were uneventful, in spite of the fact that their beat took them as far as Zeebruge. It was a different story on the 28th. That day Fighter Command flew 321 sorties, shot down 22 enemy aircraft (severely damaging six more, according to *Luftwaffe* records), and lost thirteen *Spitfires*, *Hurricanes*, and *Defiants*. Most squadrons flew two patrols; the Canadians flew three (as did Nos. 213, 229, and 616 Squadrons). The hard-working James Howitt took part in all three, including one flight of two hours and five minutes. Flight Lieutenant Miller also participated in all three; his longest patrol was two hours and twenty minutes, and another was only five minutes less than that. Clearly the *Hurricane* pilots were wringing the maximum endurance from their machines.[11]

The squadron had flown down to Manston at 5:30 a.m. and had taken off immediately after receiving their orders. At 6:40 a.m. Miller saw a dogfight in progress some three miles inland. He flew toward the engagement, but was himself attacked by a *Bf 109*. Miller evaded the enemy, attacked in turn, and knocked a few holes in it before the *Hurricane's* engine packed up; his main fuel tank was dry. By the time Miller had restarted the *Merlin* his opponent was gone; he was credited with one enemy aircraft damaged.

The ten *Hurricanes* returned to Manston, refuelled and re-armed, and shortly afterward were off again for a mid-day patrol.[12]   There was considerable cloud over Ostend, and in descending through some of it the section led by Miller, five aircraft in all, became separated from the others. They sighted a *Ju 88* and chased it

11. Ellis (see note 3), pp. 212-213 and Howitt documents (diary and logbook). Miller logbook for his flying times.

12. The timing of this patrol is not clearly stated in the records. The Squadron Operational Record Book gives times up and down as 11:30 to 12:30; two of the three Combat Reports filed give the time of the ensuing action as 11:15-11:35 a.m., while McKnight's Combat Report gives the time of the air battle as being 12:35 a.m. Nor do sources agree on the length of the patrol itself; Howitt records flying forty minutes on this occasion, while Miller logs one hour and fifty minutes!

briefly, but it disappeared into cloud.

Miller then spotted twelve *Bf 109's* flying in loose formation. He led his *Hurricanes* in an attack on the leading enemy machines; his Combat Report describes the next few moments:

> I singled out the leader and gave him a burst of approx. 5 sec from slightly above and from his beam. He appeared to go out of control and I looked around to see the sky filled with ME 109s. Turning to avoid three that were attacking me, I found myself out of control in a cloud. I regained control at 500 ft approx. and returned to base.

The little formation had been "bounced" in its turn by about sixty Messerschmitts just as the *Hurricanes* were committed to the dive on the original twelve. In those few seconds Pilot Officers Deacon and Jones were shot down. The latter was killed; Deacon's experiences bear telling in his own words. He had seen the *Bf 109's* coming and had actually broken round into their formation:

> The only way I could see to get at them in their defensive circle was to come into their circle, shoot quickly, and get out. Well, I shot quickly but so did the Hun behind me. I was hit in the oil line and with oil pouring back in my face shut off the engine, pulled the hatch back, threw off the escape hatch, undid my harness, and dove for the coast hoping to crash land on the beach or jump if the machine caught fire. Just made it to the coast, pulled back on the stick and went almost straight in.
>
> Came to in the garden of a hospital to be patched up and find out that Belgium had capitulated. Got into civilian clothes and after a few days in the Ostend, Middlekirk, Dunkirk area got to Antwerp. Went to the American Embassy but could get no help. Asked that they take my home address and write my father which they never did. Was taken a P.O.W. a few days later while in a hospital having stitches taken out of my face cuts and my leg cleaned up where I had been hit.[13]

Pilot Officer Turner engaged a *Bf 109* which seemed to be using its 20-mm cannon only. He outmanoeuvred it and delivered two bursts of three seconds duration at a range of 150 yards. The Messerschmitt went down in flames; Turner escaped into clouds and

13. Letter to the author, May 6th, 1980. Deacon meant that he had visited the American Legation in Antwerp; the Embassy itself was in Brussels.

returned to base.

The third Combat Report filed was that submitted by Pilot Officer McKnight, who had accompanied Miller in the first attack. He fired on a *'109* which was turning away; its engine stopped and the enemy fighter dived into the sea. At this point his own *Hurricane* was hit by a *'109* coming in from the port quarter, disabling his oil and coolant system. McKnight dived into the clouds, closely pursued by several Messerschmitts. He reached Manston after "a determined and sustained chase by the enemy".[14]

On May 28th No. 242 Squadron received its first reinforcements. Flight Lieutenant G.H.F. Plinston, an English pilot and veteran of service with No. 607 Squadron in France, arrived to fill the Flight Commander's position that had been vacant since the death of Sullivan. The other new man was Pilot Officer Gordon McKenzie Stewart of Stratford, Ontario, who had been granted a Short Service Commission in the RAF on January 14th, 1939 (the same day as Grassick and Turner), and had also served in No. 607 Squadron. These two men flew with No. 242 the following day as the Dunkirk air war became even hotter.

The Germans had awakened to the fact that the British Expeditionary Force was slipping through their fingers. Two enemy air fleets were now intent on closing down *Dynamo*. From noon until 8:00 p.m. of May 29th there was scarcely a break in the air attacks, and on five occasions the *Luftwaffe* achieved major concentrations of both bombers and fighters over Dunkirk. Sadly, on two of these occasions there were breaks in RAF fighter cover; the patrols had doubled in size from the 28th, being flown by from 24 to 44 aircraft, but the number of patrols themselves had declined. Even with this new method the *Hurricane* and *Spitfire* pilots frequently found themselves outnumbered, and were enmeshed in fighter-vs-fighter combats before they could reach the German bombers. Nineteen RAF fighters were lost that day; the enemy claimed to have shot down sixty-eight and admitted the loss of eighteen aircraft. Statistics

14. Such is the account as given in McKnight's Combat Report. Stan Turner tells a slightly different story By his recollection, he fired at a shape in the clouds which turned out to be McKnight's *Hurricane*, blowing the sump pump off. Back at Manston McKnight angrily confronted his friend, then broke down with laughter. Mistaken identity was not uncommon in air battles; if this report is accurate then McKnight drafted his account to protect his friend.

suggest a draw, but in fact the Germans suffered a major defeat; air power and artillery fire had failed to halt the evacuation. On this day 50,331 soldiers were landed in Britain.

About 4:30 p.m. nine pilots led by Flight Lieutenant Plinston took off from Biggin Hill to carry out a medium height (10,000 feet) patrol with No. 229 (*Hurricane*) Squadron. From Manston they flew in company with Nos. 64 and 610 (*Spitfire*) Squadrons to the patrol area. At about 5:15 p.m. No. 242 was "bounced" by some twenty *Bf 109's*.

Pilot Officer MacQueen lost his leader in a turn. Spotting a *'109* on a *Hurricane's* tail, he did a quarter attack and let go with an eight-second burst at 200 yards. The Messerschmitt began to smoke and lose altitude. "Someone was shooting at me," wrote MacQueen, "so I broke away and came back to Hawkinge." He was credited with one "probably destroyed".

Pilot Officer Stan Turner also observed a *Hurricane* beset by a *'109*, attacked the enemy fighter, and saw it spin down, smoking. He was fired at by another *'109* but turned the tables and gave it a burst. His adversary went down vertically. There were still plenty of Messerschmitts around, and Turner had to manoeuvre to escape one; Flight Lieutenant Plinston shot another off his tail.

Willie McKnight, the rising star of No. 242, was about to attack a *'109* in company with a second *Hurricane* when a Messerschmitt appeared on the tail of the latter. His Combat Report takes up the story:

> I turned sharp right and opened fire at point blank range, the enemy rolling over on his side and diving into the sea from a height of about 5000 feet. Turning away I dived on a Me 109 chasing a Hurricane and after a very short burst he began smoking and dived steeply for the shore. I followed but was unable to catch him and on turning to return I sighted a Do.17 above and to my right. I climbed sharply and attacked from the port rear quarter. My first burst disabled his port engine and [with] my last burst he began smoking and crashed about 9½ miles E. of Dunkerque. My ammunition being expended I returned to base.

McKnight may have used his bullets on more than enemy aircraft. According to the citation to his Distinguished Flying Cross, the young Albertan completed this sortie by strafing a railway being used to move up German artillery, inflicting many casualties. It is possible, however, that the strafing incident occurred during a patrol on the evening of the 29th when no enemy aircraft were seen; such is the theory advanced by Wing Commander Hitchins in *The All Canadian Squadron*. Neither in McKnight's Combat Report nor in his logbook is any reference made to attacking ground targets during the Dunkirk operation.[15]

Pilot Officer Grassick, leading Blue Section, had engaged a *Bf 109* which had dived below him. He fired two short bursts and one long one, and the Messerschmitt began smoking. Grassick followed it down until it went into the sea. He then saw another enemy aircraft, apparently crippled, flying east. He fired at it until he had expended all his ammunition. Grassick was credited with one German fighter destroyed and one damaged.

Yet another *Bf 109* fell afoul of Pilot Officer Latta, who subsequently was credited with a "probable". His was a dramatic fight, as his Combat Report indicates:

> While patrolling between Dunkirk and Nieuport in company with No. 229 Squadron at 10,000 feet we were attacked by approx. 25 ME 109s from slightly above. In the ensuing dogfight I got on the tail of an enemy machine which was executing a climbing left hand turn. The attack was delivered from dead astern and after a burst of approx. 12 secs black smoke appeared coming from his engine and the machine went into a dive. I followed it down to 2,000 feet when it disappeared in the mist still diving and apparently on fire. During the combat my undercarriage was struck and one wheel dropped partially out. I was unable to get it either up or down and had to land with one wheel down. The undercarriage and one wing was damaged.

It had been a most successful trip—five enemy aircraft destroyed, three probably destroyed, and two damaged, all without loss to the squadron. In addition to these, Pilot Officer Howitt had taken a shot at a *'109*, and although he considered the incident inconclusive, John Latta informed him that the enemy fighter had been destroyed.[16] Events would prevent Howitt from compiling a Combat Report or having the claim investigated. No. 229 Squadron had also

---

15. See Appendix "A" for the text of the citation, evidently compiled by his Commanding Officer immediately after the events described.

16. Howitt logbook and diary.

inflicted some punishment (including a *Bf 109* destroyed by a CAN/RAF member of that unit, Pilot Officer R.R. Smith), but at least five of their *Hurricanes* had been hit. No one had seen the *Spitfires*, although No. 610 Squadron had engaged several '109's at 25,000 feet, shooting down four for the loss of two of their own.

That evening No. 242 provided six pilots for another patrol. On taking off from Manston Pilot Officer Howitt (L1756) left his propeller in coarse pitch, failed to gain altitude, and crashed into a *Blenheim* parked at the edge of the field. He sustained injuries which effectively ended his tour with the squadron and would lead eventually to the resignation of his commission. Pilot Officer Stansfeld returned early with engine troubles. The remaining four aircraft were airborne for an hour and 45 minutes. Upon completing their patrol McKnight, Grassick, and MacQueen flew directly to Biggin Hill while Pilot Officer Stewart landed at Manston.

Again on the 30th No. 242 Squadron carried out two patrols over Dunkirk and Furnes in company with No. 229 Squadron.[17] Its role was to provide high cover to Nos. 64 and 610 Squadrons which were to attack bombers harassing British troops and ships—a curious reversal of roles from the 29th. Eight *Hurricanes* were mustered for the first patrol and seven for the second, but no enemy aircraft were seen on either occasion. On this day, in fact, the weather favoured the British, with low cloud at 300 feet over France curtailing *Luftwaffe* operations.[18]

17. Such, at least, is the account given in the Squadron Diary. Flight Lieutenant Miller recorded *four* sorties this day in his logbook.

18. In the period of the Dunkirk evacuation the Grassick logbook is again inconsistent with other records, suggesting that it was maintained irregularly. The following illustrates how his logbook is at variance with the Squadron Operational Record Book:

Date	Grassick Logbook	Squadron ORB
May 29, 1940	one *Bf 109* destroyed	one *Bf 109* destroyed
		one *Bf 109* damaged
May 30, 1940	one *Bf 109* "confirmed"	
	one *Bf 109* "unconfirmed"	—————
May 31, 1940	—————	one *Bf 109* damaged
June 2, 1940	one *Bf 109* destroyed	no record available

It should be remembered that No. 11 Group reported *no* victories for May 30th. The discrepancies in the records are great and virtually unexplainable. Normally

No. 242 Sqdn Hurricane LE.X in France. (A.W. Taylor)

No. 242 Sqdn road convoy halts en route from Chateaudun to St. Nazaire.
(A.W. Taylor)

Jack Cowling (American member of No. 242) rests with other exhausted ground crew during the evacuation from France, June 1940.

(A.W. Taylor)

Champagne, the French puppy that No. 242 brought back from France en route to England.

(A.W. Taylor)

No. 242 Sqdn ground crew on board ship during the evacuation from France. In foreground, Jack Cowling, D. Rice (back to camera), and G. Tyler.

(A.W. Taylor)

No. 242 personnel back from France at Falmouth, Cornwall, June 1940, including E.T. Cameron (left centre) and Sgt 'Daddy' Roussel (right). (A.W. Taylor)

After its return from France No. 242 Sqdn was stationed at Coltishall where this sunset picture was taken in August 1940. (N.K. Stansfeld)

P/O N.K. Stansfeld stands in front of his Hurricane at Coltishall, August 1940.
(N.K. Stansfeld)

The dispersal hut at Coltishall. (N.K. Stansfeld)

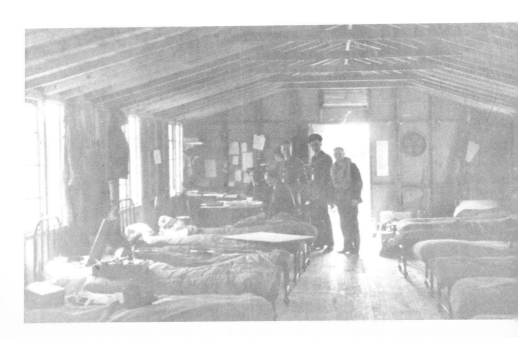

Two shots of No. 242 ground crew at Coltishall. (*Left, l to r*): T. Galbraith, L.L. Taverner, H. Galbraith, unknown (English). (*Right*): L.L. Taverner, G. Tyler, unknown, H. Galbraith. (A.W. Taylor)

AC.1 H.S. Jeff at work on LE.G.
(A.W. Taylor)

A.W. Taylor, one of No. 242's ground crew who supplied many of the photos for this book.
(A.W. Taylor)

Two more groundcrew members, A.A. Martin and C.T. Gibbons, are photographed on LE.G's wing.   (A.W. Taylor)

S/L D.R.S. Bader assumed command of No. 242 on 24 June 1940. Here he is photographed (second from left, with pipe) with some squadron pilots. McKnight is in centre with back to camera.   (N.K. Stansfeld)

The puppy Champagne, brought back from France, was No. 242's mascot until killed by a truck at Coltishall. The mourners (*bottom*) consist of Martin, Rice, unknown (English), Cummings (English), unknown (English), Sleigh, and Cameron. (A.W. Taylor)

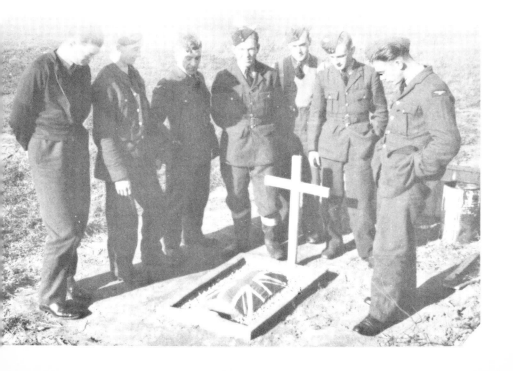

Two Battle of Britain scenes show the Duxford operations room and armourers reloading the guns of a Hurricane.   (IWM)

The squadron was placed at "half hour readiness" at 11:30 a.m. on the 31st, but weather continued to restrict operations by both air forces until mid-afternoon. At 3:55 p.m. eight *Hurricanes*, led by Flight Lieutenant Plinston, took off to join their customary companions, Nos. 229, 64, and 610 Squadrons, for a patrol along their usual beat. No. 229 was flying the low patrol at 8,000 feet with No. 242 at 12,000 feet; No. 610 was stepped up at 15,000 feet and No. 64 at 22,000 feet.

The patrol itself was uneventful. After its completion they went looking for an enemy observation balloon south of Nieuport that had been spotting for German guns bombarding the evacuation area. They failed to locate it, but on the return flight No. 242 intercepted a formation of nine enemy bombers off Dunkirk, attacked, and forced the Germans to turn back. Once again it was a dramatic fight.

Plinston chased a *Ju 88* out to sea, put the rear gunner out of action, and finished his ammunition in two long bursts. The bomber began to smoke and turned toward the coast; Plinston was credited with one "destroyed".

As Plinston had singled out his target, Pilot Officer MacQueen had gone after another bomber—either a *Ju 88* or a *Do 17*. At a range of 400 yards he pushed the "tit", firing until he was within 50 yards of the target. At that point he ran out of ammunition. He observed Plinston's '*88* going down, and then had to break for home.

Meanwhile, Pilot Officer Stansfeld had spotted a *Bf 110*, presumably part of an escort force for the bombers. He pounced from the rear port quarter. The '*110* dived, but the Canadian was not shaken off. At 350 yards Stansfeld started firing and kept it up for a full six seconds. The starboard engine of the enemy machine disintegrated and the '*110* crashed on the beach below.

During this action the other *Hurricane* pilots were attacking the bombers. Pilot Officer McKnight had lagged behind his formation. He climbed for a better position, then dived to join in the melee. As he did so some 25 or 30 *Bf 110's* also plunged into the fray. He brought his sights to bear on the leading enemy aircraft, hit

logbooks were checked monthly and endorsed as being correct by Flight and Squadron Commanders; in Grassick's case such endorsements are lacking for May and June 1940. This was probably due to the intense level of air fighting at the time, and to the extensive turnover in senior personnel late in June.

it, and forced it to swerve. That broke up the Messerschmitt formation. McKnight switched his fire to a second *'110*. Abruptly the two *Bf 110's* collided and went down in flames. "Being out of ammunition, I ceased the attack and returned to base", wrote McKnight at the conclusion of his Combat Report.

At 7:25 p.m. six pilots took off for another balloon search, once more with Plinston in the lead. Soon after reaching Dunkirk (8:10 p.m.) Plinston saw some enemy aircraft to the southeast and took off in pursuit of them. Another formation came into sight to the south and then a gaggle of fifteen *Bf 109's* appeared to the north. Plinston turned the formation toward this last group of opponents. As he did so the *Hurricanes* were attacked from the rear by some thirty high-flying *Bf 109's*.

The odds were all wrong, but most of the *Hurricane* pilots fought their way free of the trap. Pilot Officer Latta fired short bursts at three different aircraft without apparent effect. He got on the tail of a fourth, delivered a ten-second burst, and saw it go down out of control into the sea. While dogfighting furiously he also observed two other Messerschmitts descending out of control.

Pilot Officer Turner engaged a *Bf 109* which he outmanoeuvred. At 150 yards he fired a five-second burst. The enemy aircraft went down out of control and crashed in the English Channel. Another *'109* was destroyed by Plinston, whose own fighter was badly shot about.

Pilot Officers Grassick and McKnight each submitted claims for a *Bf 109* damaged. Grassick's victim had begun to smoke when Grassick was "bounced" by more Messerschmitts, from which he escaped with the greatest difficulty. McKnight, too, was unable to press home his attack due to the number of enemy machines about. No. 229 Squadron reported that four German fighters had been shot down, although only those three credited to Plinston, Latta, and Turner could be positively identified. In this action No. 242 suffered another loss; Pilot Officer Stewart, who had joined the unit on the 28th, was shot down and killed in Hurricane P2732.[19]

19. James J. Halley, *Royal Air Force Aircraft, P1000 to P9999* (Tonbridge, 1978) records two aircraft, P2732 and P2884, as being lost on May 31st. The nature of the records, by Halley's own admission, are sometimes vague. P2884 may have been Plinston's machine, written off after battle damage, or may have been on strength of another squadron.

The heaviest aerial fighting during *Dynamo* occurred on June 1st. From first light onward the *Luftwaffe* launched raid upon raid, bombing not only the harbour and beaches but also ships en route back to England. Fighter Command flew eight sweeps in three- and four-squadron strength; additional patrols were flown over the Goodwin Sands (near the English coast) by *Ansons* and *Hudsons* of Coastal Command. Combats were furious and continuous; by evening the RAF had lost 31 aircraft; *Luftwaffe* losses were ten fighters and nineteen bombers destroyed and thirteen aircraft seriously damaged.[20]

No. 242's major encounter came at 4:35 p.m., when McKnight and Stansfeld met fifteen *Ju 87's* dive-bombing ships just off the crucial beaches. McKnight attacked one which had entered its dive; it never pulled out. Climbing back, he closed in below and behind a second "Stuka" and gave it a "squirt". This machine emitted smoke, then plummetted into the Channel. A third *Ju 87* took some hits and streamed smoke, but then vanished into clouds. McKnight finished his ammunition on yet another *Ju 87* that appeared to be badly hit. He then carried out a number of feint attacks, driving off several enemy machines. He was credited with two confirmed victories and two "probables".[21]

Noel Stansfeld attacked a *Ju 87*. His target dropped its bombs, then absorbed a ten-second burst. It rolled over on its back, but Stansfeld lost sight of it as he passed. He was credited with one "probably destroyed".

While these combats were in progress at about 2,500 feet, other members of No. 242 at 5,000 feet were "bounced" by fourteen *Bf 109's*. Flight Lieutenant Miller pulled under one and fired a three-second deflection burst. The *'109* rolled part-way onto its back and passed over the *Hurricane*. Miller repeated the process on another *'109* but saw no result. Although he was confident that the

---

20. Ellis, (see note 3), p. 243.

21. McKnight later stated that the Royal Navy confirmed the "probables" as "destroyed"; see "Local Pilot Bags 14 Nazi Craft", Calgary *Herald*, October 2nd, 1940. This is repeated in Sir Harry Brittain, *Come the Three Corners* (London, 1940), p. 86 and Peter J. Field, *Canada's Wings* (London, 1942), p. 36. Nevertheless, McKnight's logbook entry for the engagement reads, "Four Ju.87—two confirmed, two unconfirmed", and his Combat Report bears no evidence of upgrading.

first Messerschmitt would not get home, he was credited with two enemy aircraft damaged.

Stan Turner had manoeuvred to face the enemy attack, delivering a seven-second burst at a '109 which dived into the sea. He then attacked two more Messerschmitts, firing a long burst into one. Turner's *Hurricane* stalled and he lost sight of his target; on recovering control he saw only one. Having used all his ammunition he returned home. He claimed "one 109 possible, one 109 probable", and was credited with a single *Bf 109* destroyed.[22]

The combats of June 1st are the last of No. 242's Dunkirk actions of which clear accounts can be assembled. The squadron flew one, possibly two patrols over the area on June 2nd; McKnight recorded a two hour and five minute sortie while Grassick logged a one hour and 30 minute flight in which he shot down a *Bf 109*; no Combat Report of the action has been located, and Grassick's victory may, in fact, be confused in his own records with an action on May 31st, documented in the Squadron ORB and Combat Reports, but not in his logbook.[23]

James Howitt, still with the unit though undergoing tests following his crash of May 29th, reported in his diary that Turner had suffered oxygen failure at 20,000 feet, causing him to spin down to a lower altitude. He recovered his senses just in time to avoid crashing.

A further patrol may have occurred on June 3rd; the Grassick logbook records one sortie over Dunkirk this day. This was almost certainly the last flight in the evacuation area; on June 4th both McKnight and Grassick recorded a patrol over Canterbury. That same day word came through that "Willie" McKnight had been

---

22. Records of CAN/RAF personnel held by DHist credit Miller with "one probable" and "one damaged", but the Combat Report bears a notation, almost certainly that of an Intelligence Officer, which assesses the claim as "two damaged". Similar evidence relates to Turner's combat. The events of June 1st are reconstructed from Combat Reports and available logbook entries; the Squadron Operational Record Book contains no entries for June 1st to 13th. Halley (see note 19) lists three *Hurricanes* (L1948, N2004, and N2424) as being on the strength of No. 242 and lost this day. The squadron sustained no losses on June 1st; the aircraft may have been transferred to other units and subsequently lost.

23. See note 18.

awarded an immediate Distinguished Flying Cross; he was invested with the decoration by King George VI on June 7th.

During the period of its operations from British bases, No. 242 had acquitted itself well. The records are not always consistent, but a minimum reckoning of the unit's achievements shows that its pilots were credited with 21 enemy machines destroyed, seven probably destroyed, and eight damaged. Most of these victories were claimed after May 26th, during Operation *Dynamo*. Losses had been heavy— six pilots killed (Graafstra, Madore, Mitchell, Jones, Stewart, and Hill), two captured (Smiley and Deacon), one wounded (Benzie), and two injured in accidents (Waterton and Howitt). The bulk of the casualties had been sustained on May 23rd and 24th, before the intense fighting accompanying *Dynamo* had commenced. The improved operational efficiency during the Dunkirk period indicated the confidence gained with experience; it might also have been due partly to Flight Lieutenant Plinston, whose previous service in France had given him much first-hand knowledge of *Luftwaffe* tactics. Offsetting this operational confidence, however, was a disturbing development. During the battles of May and early June every pilot of Flying Officer rank had been lost in action, leaving No. 242 bereft of middle-echelon officers. The squadron was reduced to the leaders (Gobeil, Miller, Plinston) and several Pilot Officers.

Throughout the period that No. 242's pilots had been in action, whether attached to other squadrons or acting as a unit, Canadian authorities had not lost interest in the experiment, although the arrival of regular RCAF formations in Britain had made No. 242 less relevant to the establishment of a Canadian presence in the war effort. No. 110 Squadron (RCAF) had reached the United Kingdom in February 1940; Nos. 1 (Fighter) and 112 (Army Co-operation) Squadrons would arrive in June 1940. Nevertheless, none of the newcomers were as yet fully operational.

On May 7th the Honourable Norman Rogers (Canada's Minister of National Defence) and Group Captain G.V. Walsh had visited the squadron. On May 30th, in the midst of the Dunkirk operation, the unit was again visited by "brass", this time by Vincent Massey and Walsh. Much more important, though, was that No. 242's fate was still in the minds of RCAF authorities in Britain. On May 15th, 1940 Group Captain Walsh had written a memorandum expressing concern that the squadron might not remain "Canadian" in content:

> The question of replacement of casualties will arise shortly. It is not known whether the Royal Air Force will be able to replace the casualties in this squadron by Canadian personnel, particularly as, under major operations, the reinforcements problem of the Royal Air Force will assume large proportions.
>
> It appears to me that there is a possibility of this Unit losing its Canadian identity, if the Royal Air Force is unable to replace casualties by Canadian personnel. It is, therefore, suggested that consideration might be given by Canada to the replacement of casualties in No. 242 (Canadian) Squadron by Royal Canadian Air Force personnel sent from Canada, in order that the Unit may retain its special identity.[24]

Walsh's concern was well founded. From May 14th to the 31st, on the Continent and over Dunkirk, No. 242 Squadron had lost fifteen pilots killed, wounded, captured, or injured. Only two pilots had been posted in—one British (Plinston) and one Canadian (Stewart, who quickly became one of the unfortunate fifteen).

Some reinforcements arrived in early June. Pilot Officer H.E. Horne, formerly of No. 615 Squadron, arrived on the 2nd. Next day brought Pilot Officers A.E. Eckford and Norman Neil Campbell, both from No. 32 Squadron. On June 6th Pilot Officers C.R. Bush (a New Zealander) and D. Crowley-Milling were posted from No. 615 to No. 242. Both would figure prominently in the history of their squadron; Crowley-Milling would make a particular impact, being remembered as a Rolls-Royce expert who knew as much about engines as the mechanics, and as having a personality so pleasing that he was regarded as an honorary Canadian. In addition to these, Pilot Atkinson and Sergeant E. Richardson joined the squadron at an uncertain date. Of these new men, only Campbell, who hailed from St. Thomas, Ontario, was Canadian. The dilution of the squadron's "Canadian content" had begun.

One might ask if Air Ministry had forgotten the commitment to making No. 242 a "Canadian" outfit. It would appear that they had, but two factors should be borne in mind. One was that relatively few CAN/RAF pilots emerged from the fighter training pipe-

---

24. Group Captain Walsh (Officer Commanding, RCAF in Britain) to Secretary, Office of the High Commissioner for Canada. See Chapter 1, note 1.

line at this time; they might have been made available to No. 242, but were in fact sent to other units.[25] The other point was the brutal reality of the situation; with a debacle in progress in France, attending to Canadian sensibilities would receive no particular consideration. The RAF had far more important things to consider than the national composition of one particular squadron.

25. From the outset the RAF had refused to post significant numbers of CAN/RAF personnel from existing squadrons, leaving No. 242 to receive "unemployed" CAN/RAF fighter pilots. That few of these were available in the spring of 1940 can be seen from reviewing other squadrons receiving such people. On May 16th Flying Officer R.A. Barton had been sent to No. 249 Squadron, then forming; on May 17th Pilot Officer C.R. Bonseigneur had been posted to No. 257 Squadron; on May 23rd Pilot Officer A.C. Cochrane reported to No. 257 and Pilot Officer R.R. Wilson was reposted to No. 56 (his former unit); on May 25th Flight Lieutenant H.R. Hamilton was switched from No. 611 to No. 85 Squadron while Pilot Officer J.E.P. Laricheliere was posted to No. 213 Squadron; on May 27th Pilot Officer J.D. Smith went to No. 73 Squadron; on June 9th Pilot Officer J.A. Milne went to No. 72 Squadron.

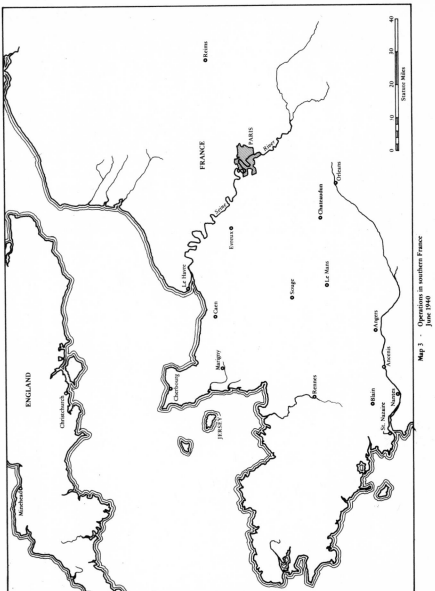

Map 3 - Operations in southern France
June 1940

France Again

With its strength partially restored, No. 242 Squadron was soon in action again, this time in one of the most confusing and frustrating situations of the war. Not all of the British Expeditionary Force had escaped through Dunkirk; two divisions and assorted ancillary formations had been operating apart from the main body of the BEF and were now stranded in France, south of the Seine River. France herself was still fighting, though her spirits were failing and her armies were shattered. British authorities hoped to keep the doomed republic in the war. To this end reinforcements were to be despatched to the Continent. These would include the leading elements of the 1st Canadian Division together with additional fighter squadrons.

On June 8th, in company with No. 17 Squadron, No. 242 flew to Le Mans to reinforce those RAF fighter squadrons still in France—Nos. 1, 73, and 501.[1] As they landed they saw a grim spectacle: a wrecked *Hurricane* beside the aerodrome. The previous day Flying

1. By coincidence, No. 17 Squadron was commanded by a Canadian member of the Royal Air Force, Squadron Leader R.I.G. MacDougall.

Officer E.J. "Cobber" Kain, a brilliant New Zealand fighter pilot and the first Commonwealth "ace" to catch the public eye, had crashed and been killed while doing aerobatics over the field. The wreckage had been left to warn others of the hazards that went with such needless antics.[2]

Later on the 8th No. 242 proceeded to Chateaudun, northwest of Orleans, where it came under No. 67 Wing. A sizable contingent of groundcrew followed by air transport; No. 271 Squadron, using two Bristol *Bombays* and one Handley-Page *Harrow* aircraft, left Biggin Hill at 1:00 p.m., carrying a total of forty-nine airmen with kit, stores, and freight. They landed at Le Mans where a *Bombay* with twenty-six men was unloaded. The others were taken on to Chateaudun and disembarked.[3] These were field servicing staff, responsible for refuelling, re-arming, and repairing aircraft. They were unable to carry out extensive inspections or rebuild seriously damaged machines; *Hurricanes* sustaining major damage would have to be replaced or abandoned. Left in England were Pilot Officers Grassick (who would follow on the 12th) and Howitt. The latter, waiting for X-rays, found that his duties now consisted of sorting the luggage and re-addressing the letters of the many aircrew who had gone missing, a task he described in his diary as "depressing".

At Chateaudun the men were housed in large bell tents—roughly ten to a tent, sleeping in a circle. Headquarters was a house just off the field. Corporal Larry Stopforth, an airframe and aero engine mechanic from Waterloo, remembers one person vividly—a friendly

---

2. Interview with P.S. Turner, September 9th, 1980.

3. No. 271 Squadron Operational Record Book. For the period of June 1st to June 13th there is no ORB for No. 242 Squadron, and entries from June 14th to the end of the month are vague. The notes that would have been the basis of a squadron diary appear to have been lost in France; the same thing happened to other squadrons fighting on the Continent at that time.

The events of this period have been reconstructed from several sources. Wing Commander Hitchins, in compiling the first history of No. 242, described his narrative as "a tentative one based upon items pieced together from other sources". He specifically mentioned Mr. Dennis Richards (Air Historical Branch, Air Ministry, and co-author of *The Royal Air Force, 1939-45*) and Sergeant Jack Cowling, an American who was a fitter with No. 242. Other of Hitchins' sources will be mentioned later. This writer has relied largely upon the earlier accounts supplemented by some new material from logbooks, letters written by squadron personnel, and recollections provided in 1980.

French guard (probably a reservist) who had a very ancient rifle and a single bullet. He kept the cartridge in his pocket, but would occasionally pull it out to show people.[4]

The day after their arrival the squadron flew to Marigny and then to Haver. From there seven *Hurricanes* carried out a patrol over Reims, on the Aisne front, protecting a French army withdrawal from German dive bombers. They were at 12,000 feet when approximately fifteen *Bf 109's* attacked them from above and out of the sun. Two in succession sprayed MacQueen's fighter (P2767), which wobbled violently. Turner radioed his friend to bale out but there was no response. He then exacted swift revenge, shooting down the *'109* that had killed MacQueen. Minutes later, Turner shot down a second *Bf 109*.[5]

The squadron returned to Chateaudun that evening. For the next three days the only records of the unit's activities are brief logbook entries. Pilot Officer McKnight's flying was noted as follows:

June 10th—OP [Offensive Patrol] Le Havre—1.45 [one hour
             and 45 minutes]
June 11th—Orbit base, 10,000 feet—20 min.
        —Escort, east of Le Havre—2.10
        —Patrol Le Havre—2.15
June 12th—Patrol base—2.00

Pilot Officer Stansfeld was equally busy, flying one patrol on the 10th, four on the 11th, and two on the 12th. It is evident from his logbook that much time was taken up each day in flying from Chateaudun to forward airfields each morning, then back to base each night. The fact that Le Havre was the focal point of operations—whether these were bomber escort sorties or standing patrols over the port—was due to a peculiar two-way flow of traffic. It was through Le Havre that reinforcements for a reconstituted British Expeditionary Force were initially landed; it was through the same port they were then evacuated. The German advance was wheeling about to the southwest, beginning a push into the Cherbourg penin-

4. L.H. Stopforth to the author, June 1980.

5. The account of this action is drawn from the Calgary *Herald* of October 2nd, 1940, and from Peter J. Field, *op. cit.* (see Chapter 2, note 2), p. 27. Both refer to an unidentified "official report", not traced by this writer.

sula.[6]

About this time Flight Lieutenant Miller fell sick and was evacuated to England.[7] He was not replaced, and this added to Squadron Leader Gobeil's burden. He now shared leadership of the unit with only one Flight Commander. No. 242's resources were becoming seriously strained.

In the early hours of June 13th the squadron was hit by further misfortune. Careless smoking started a fire in one of the bell tents. Crowley-Milling recalled the event:

> I woke up . . . to find the whole of the roof of the tent on fire, only to dash out in my pyjamas to be greeted full down the front with a fire extinguisher. The tent burned right down and some of our clothes. We had to beg and borrow and do the best we could, but the squadron missed a patrol as a result.[8]

No. 73 Squadron's records note merely that the Canadians had suffered a fire which left them "rather scantily clad". No. 242 had been detailed to escort some *Battles*, but No. 73 was given this task while the Canadians re-assembled their kit. The operation was scrubbed by weather. No. 242 flew very little that day, although "Slim" Grassick logged two hours and 20 minutes in two patrols.

By the evening of June 13th the German advance was beginning to threaten Chateaudun. At 9:00 p.m. the squadrons there received orders to move back. Air Marshal A.S. Barratt, commanding the RAF in France, planned to concentrate his air forces in the area of

6. See Chapter 2, note 1. In his 1941 narrative, Wing Commander Hitchins surmised that No. 242's work had been to provide cover for the evacuation of the troops from Le Havre, to patrol the lower Seine and St. Valery-en-Caux as protection against dive bombers, to escort the bombers on their missions, and to keep sections at readiness or in the air on aerodrome defence. Logbook entries by McKnight, Stansfeld, and Grassick indicate more limited duties—patrols over Le Havre, airfield protection, and limited escort work.

7. Miller returned to flying in September 1940, when he took an instructor's course prior to being posted to Canada. He ended the war as a Wing Commander in charge of No. 525 (Transport) Squadron. Later he led No. 426 (Transport) Squadron. He was awarded the Air Force Cross in September 1945. Transferring to the RCAF, he retired in 1964 as a Group Captain.

8. Air Marshal Sir Denis Crowley-Milling to the author, November 13th, 1980.

Nantes, Rennes, Angers, and Saumar, and to resume operations from these bases. They were so crowded with French aircraft, however, that temporary arrangements had to be made for some RAF units.

Nos. 1 and 242 Squadrons were instructed to send their ground crews immediately to Souge, while the aircraft, pilots, and rear party were to remain at Chateaudun to operate on the 14th; after that they were to fly to Caen and await new aerodrome facilities. Before this plan could be put into effect, the ground situation deteriorated still further. French defences everywhere had been breached; German troops were across the Seine in strength. Paris had fallen, and the French generals were demanding that their government seek an armistice. Clearly there was no hope of maintaining a foothold on the Continent, so it was soon decided that the only viable policy was to pull out as quickly as possible.

When the order to move came through on the evening of the 13th, there was no transport available. As rumours circulated of impending German paratroop descents, the RAF personnel rounded up a collection of trucks, most in disrepair, and an airfield beacon trailer. At 11:00 a.m. on the 14th the road convoy departed. As they drove away, Corporal Stopforth noticed their French guard—the reservist with only one bullet—sitting on his doorstep, wearing civilian clothes, watching impassively as the vehicles lumbered past. The men had few rations; someone with foresight had filled two sacks with carrots.

They reached Ancenis that evening and remained overnight. On the morning of the 15th the ground personnel moved eastward again, to Angers. French civilians cheered them on this occasion, thinking that they were troops heading for the front. Upon arrival at their destination they were ordered to turn back to Nantes, where they were briefly reunited with their squadrons. That night, however, responding to vague instructions that seemed to come from No. 67 Wing HQ, No. 242's groundcrew embarked in trucks, unbeknown to either the Commanding Officer or the Adjutant. They proceeded to St. Nazaire at the mouth of the Loire River, one of the last evacuation ports for British personnel escaping from the Continent.

The loading and sailing of ships was punctuated by sporadic *Luftwaffe* raids; Stopforth remembers two *Bf 110's* circling in and out of low clouds while their rear gunners peppered the area.

No. 242's personnel remained outside the port until a vessel was ready. There was some talk of boarding the liner *Lancastria*, but ultimately they were grouped with another batch of RAF airmen who were under the supervision of an officer. An acquaintance nevertheless invited Stopforth to come aboard the *Lancastria*, but the offer was declined. By such incidents did No. 242's groundcrew escape one of the worst sea disasters of the war. On June 17th the *Lancastria*, crammed with over 5,000 military and civilian evacuees, was sunk by German bombers, with a loss of more than 2,800 lives.[9]

Meanwhile, in scenes reminiscent of those Albert Taylor had witnessed at Boulogne a month earlier, NAAFI personnel opened crates of cigarettes and chocolate, inviting everyone to help themselves. Aircraftman S.G. Stopford of Vancouver recounted how the canteen was "disposing of their entire stock of merchandise and there were some marvellous bargains—i.e. writing materials, razors, razor blades, shaving soap, soap, etc., etc."[10]

At the dockside a strange, poignant parting occurred. Upon their arrival in France, No. 242 had been assigned as an interpreter a British veteran of the First World War. The man had married and settled in France between the wars, had followed the squadron through its confusing moves, and was now invited to accompany them back to England. He refused, preferring to stay with his family and take his chances under German occupation.[11]

While waiting for a vessel the groundcrew acquired a mascot, a black and white terrier pup that was dubbed "Champagne". When the airmen embarked on the Polish liner *Sobieski*, Aircraftman Ken Fisher of Victoria smuggled the animal aboard in the pocket of his greatcoat. The dog was to have a short career with No. 242; at Coltishall it died under the wheels of a truck.

Crowded to capacity and beyond, the *Sobieski* left St. Nazaire

9. See Charles Hocking, *Dictionary of Disasters at Sea During the Age of Steam* (London, 1969), Volume 1, p. 412.

10. S.G. Stopford to the author, June 30th, 1980.

11. Larry Stopforth and Albert Taylor were both present during the fiasco of June 1940, but disagree in their reminiscences on the subject of the interpreter. Stopforth has stated that the man went with them to St. Nazaire; Taylor maintains that he left the squadron much earlier—probably at Chateaudun. The timing of his departure is less important than his painful decision to remain in France.

at 10:00 a.m. on the 16th. Most of the men had been crammed below decks. The liner sailed out in the middle of an air raid. For the men in the hold it was a terrifying experience; the hammering of the ship's light guns reverberated through the hull, which amplified the racket. Several times the airmen believed that the *Sobieski* had been hit. In fact, the raiders had little chance to take aim; RAF fighters and British anti-aircraft guns put up stiff resistance. The airmen reached Falmouth safely on the morning of June 18th. From there they were transported to Weston-super-Mare, on to Duxford, and finally to Coltishall, where they were reunited with those tradesmen who had remained in England.

In the course of the evacuation No. 242's groundcrew had witnessed terrible events. France had fallen apart and her society had disintegrated before their eyes. Some civilians had been sympathetic; others had reviled them for what was perceived to be the desertion of an ally.

An army in retreat is often an object of contempt. One of the most heartening aspects of this retreat was the reception accorded the servicemen upon their arrival in Britain. In port they found barracks ready, though many preferred to sleep outdoors on their mattresses, having liked the experience of living under canvas. The civil populace willingly helped feed the men until trains could move them elsewhere.

Meanwhile, the pilots and rear party of No. 242 had their work cut out for them. British fighters had several tasks to perform—including escorting bombers and patrolling the Seine estuary as well as the vicinity of Evreux, where the German penetration was most severe. The Canadians contributed to some of these operations, notably offensive patrols, which dominated the McKnight, Grassick, and Stansfeld logbook entries. On June 14th McKnight recorded considerable action and two squadron moves:

> June 14—Raid on aerodrome—.35
> —Chateaudun-Le Mans—1.45
> —Patrol Seine to Paris—2.20—12 ME.109s Attacked—
> 12 Destroyed—2 Personal Conf.
> —Le Mans-Nantes—1.00

The air battle referred to by McKnight is mentioned by other pilots, although their reports do not agree fully with one another. Noel Stansfeld noted the move to Le Mans in his logbook, as well as a subsequent patrol in which he shot down a *Bf 109*, but gave the date as being June 13th! Crowley-Milling, on the other hand, put the date as being the 14th, and recorded enemy casualties as six destroyed. He personally engaged a Messerschmitt but lost it in clouds. The story of this action is supplemented by an "official report", untraced, but quoted in secondary sources. According to this unidentified account, the battle commenced at 9,000 feet, twelve enemy machines were destroyed, and the last was shot down just short of the German lines.[12]

Pilot Officer Grassick was also active that day, flying a total of two hours and 55 minutes. His moves from base to base did not coincide precisely with those recorded by McKnight; the Londoner had logged himself as going to Le Mans on the 13th and to Nantes on the 15th; he was almost certainly on the patrol that engaged the *Bf 109's* between Le Mans and Paris. The differences in logbook entries suggest that the pilots did not always change bases in squadron strength; they may sometimes have transferred to new airfields by flights at different times. On the other hand, the irregular maintenance of records characterized this hectic campaign, and has led to several instances of erroneous or questionable documents.

Noel Stansfeld experienced an incident which his logbook dates as June 14th; it may have occurred on the 15th. He and some comrades had flown to Rennes, from where six of them undertook a patrol. They were heading eastward under scattered cumulous cloud when Stansfeld saw some *Bf 109's* below the *Hurricanes*. He waggled his wings and the Canadians started down to attack, only to be jumped and scattered by roughly twenty more *109's*. Suddenly he found himself alone, lost, and without maps. He had no idea how to regain his base.

Stansfeld selected what appeared to be a good landing spot in a field close to a village. The place was not as well-suited as he had guessed, for he narrowly missed dropping over the bank of a stream as he rolled to a stop. From all directions French peasants converged upon him, waving assorted ancient rifles and muskets. They did not

---

12. Crowley-Milling to the author, November 13th, 1980; Field, *op.cit.* (see Chapter 2, note 2), p. 37; Calgary *Herald*, October 2nd, 1940. It seems incredible that a dozen *Bf 109's* could be shot down by a like number of *Hurricanes* of inferior performance. Even six appears unlikely, but over-claiming in the course of close combat was common in all air forces. This writer has been unable to determine which pilots other than Stansfeld and McKnight inflicted casualties on the other enemy aircraft.

Pilots of No. 242 Squadron pose by S/L Bader's Hurricane, September 1940.
(*l to r*): P/O's D. Crowley-Milling, H.N. Tamblyn, P.S. Turner, Sgt. J.E. Saville
(on wing), P/O's N.N. Campbell, W.L. McKnight, S/L Bader, F/L G.E. Ball,
P/O's M.G. Homer, M.K. Brown. (IWM)

Ball, Bader, and McKnight eye the painting on the Hurricane's nose. This motif
was not solely on S/L Bader's aircraft but carried on most No. 242 Squadron
Hurricanes. (IWM)

S/L D.R.S. Bader. Note the squadron leader's pennant painted beneath the cockpit.　　　(IWM)

F/L G.E. Ball, an Englishman who joined No. 242 as a flight commander in June 1940.　　　(IWM)

P/O H.N. Tamblyn, a Canadian who joined the squadron in August 1940.　　　(IWM)

P/O M.K. Brown, one of the original squadron members, who, wounded in May 1940, rejoined No. 242 in July.　　　(IWM)

Probably the outstanding Canadian fighter pilot of the first half of the war, P/O W.L. McKnight, who was credited with 16½ victories before his death in action on 12 January 1941. (IWM)

P/O N.N. Campbell, a Canadian who was killed in action on 17 October 1940. (IWM)

P/O P.S. Turner, an excellent fighter pilot and leader, who had a most active and successful wartime career. (IWM)

Two English members of No. 242, P/O M.G. Homer who was posted to the squadron on 21 September and killed in action on 27 September 1940, and P/O D. Crowley-Milling who was to become Air Marshal Sir Denis Crowley-Milling in the post-war RAF. (IWM)

A Spitfire of No. 19 Squadron, based at Duxford in September 1940.   (IWM)

LAC C.T. Gibbons with a distinctively marked Hurricane, possibly P/O N.N. Campbell's. Brickhill attributes this marking to P/O N. Hart.   (A.W. Taylor)

Two shots of No. 242 Squadron in formation, October 1940.   (IWM)

Two of the three pilots from the Royal Navy who flew with No. 242 during the Battle of Britain, Sub-Lieutenants R.J. Cork and R.E. Gardner. (Una Grassick via PAC)

P/O's Stan Turner, Willie McKnight, and Bob Grassick in a relaxed moment. (Una Grassick via PAC)

P/O N. Hart, a Canadian pilot who joined No. 242 in July and was killed in November 1940.

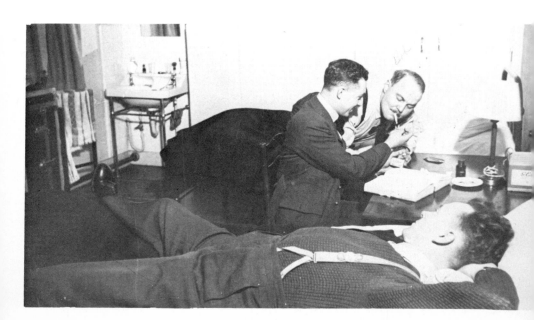

F/O D. Crowley-Milling holds the shattered windscreen of his Hurricane. (Una Grassick via NMC)

No. 242 pilots ham for the camera. (*Above, l to r*): Bull, Grassick (pointing), Bader, and Turner. (*Bottom*): Bader, Dibnah, McKnight, Cryderman, Tamblyn (seated).
(Una Grassick via PAC)

Photos taken December 1940 of No. 242 Sqdn pilots and officers (*top*) and all squadron personnel (*bottom*). Names (*l to r*) in top photo are: (*front row*): F/O W.L. McKnight, Sgt E. Richardson, F/L G.E. Ball, S/L D.R.S. Bader, F/L P.S. Turner, Sgt. L.R. Truman, F/O H.N. Tamblyn; (*back row*): P/O D.J. McKenna, R.H. Dibnah, F/O J.B. Latta, P/O A.W. Smith, F/O P.D. MacDonald (Adj), F/O D. Crowley-Milling, F/O L.E. Price, F/O M.K. Brown, F/O E.O. Lang, F/O N.D. Edmond, P/O J.A. Deschamps, P/O H.L.D. Kemp.

(Una Grassick via PAC)

F/O W.L. McKnight used his experience as a medical student to assist him in selecting and painting a personal insignia for his aircraft as seen in these photos taken in December 1940. (C.I.R. Arthur)

P/O N.D. Edmond, S/L Bader, F/O McKnight, F/L Ball, and F/O Brown in a winter scene, ca. January 1940.

P/O N.D. Edmond and his groundcrew.
(Una Grassick via NMC)

P/O A.W. Smith and F/L Hugh Tamblyn at Martlesham Heath, February 1941.
(Noel H. Barlow)

P/O J.B. Latta, one of the original members of the squadron, who was killed in action, January 1941.
(Noel H. Barlow)

A Stirling over France with Hurricane escort. It was on such offensive operations that No. 242 lost some of its best pilots.   (IWM)

Sgt E.H.C. Kee, P/O H.L.D. Kemp, Sgt J.R. Pollard, P/O B.A. Rogers, Sgt E.
Richardson, F/O H.N. Tamblyn.   (Una Grassick via NMC)

Hurricane over the Thames, early 1941. (C.I.R. Arthur)

Groundcrew of No. 242. (*Front row, l to r*): Dale Stevens, Cameron, unknown, unknown, RCAF unknown, Tyler, unknown (English), K. Fisher, Deloume, Southall, H. Galbraith. (*Top*): RCAF unknown, Jeffs, Godfrey, T. Galbraith, Coupland, Dyer, unknown, A.W. Taylor, Lloyd Hall, RCAF unknown, Baines, Sleigh, unknown. (C.I.R. Arthur)

believe that he was a British pilot, and he could not clearly explain his presence. It appeared that he was going to be arrested if he was lucky and shot if he was not.

At last one man pushed through the crowd and effected a quick rescue. This person spoke good English; he had once been a cook in England. A brass compass and a Michelin road map were produced and the young Canadian was given directions to a French airfield where he might refuel. First of all he had to take off from his improvised landing strip. The French beat down some of the wheat. Stansfeld then stood on the brakes, revved up the engine until he was in danger of nosing over, released the brakes, and took off.

Having secured some gasoline, Stansfeld set course for Rennes, but again lost his way. Below was a railway line on which a train was carrying British troops and equipment. He resolved to land beside the tracks and ask for further directions. This time he was less fortunate. As the *Hurricane* touched down it ran into a ditch, wiping out the undercarriage. A deafening roar filled the cockpit as an emergency horn went off. Somebody rushed up to render assistance; Stansfeld's first act was to borrow a knife and disconnect the horn. The aircraft was a write-off; he hitch-hiked from Blain (where he had crashed) to Nantes the next morning. No. 242 had by that time concentrated there for the defence of nearby St. Nazaire.[13]

No. 242's move to Nantes seems to have been conducted over two days, June 14th and 15th. They shared the Nantes/Bourgon airfield with Nos. 1 and 73 Squadrons, flying local airfield protection sorties and numerous patrols over St. Nazaire itself. Available log-books indicate that over the period of June 15th to 17th the pilots conducted two or three sorties daily, each lasting an average of ninety minutes, although some extended to more than two hours.

Confusion reigned at Nantes airfield. Without their ground-crew, pilots had to refuel, re-arm, and service their own aircraft. There were fears that fifth-columnists might sabotage the fighters, so aircrew slept under the wings of the *Hurricanes*.[14] Fortunately,

13. Stansfeld logbook, interview of November 20th, 1980, and Vancouver *Sun*, August 8th, 1940.

14. The extent of these fears is brought out by Stan Turner's statement, years afterward, that enemy agents had gotten onto the airfield one night and turned

the level of enemy air activity was low; the raids experienced by No. 242's groundcrew in the port were not the norm, although the bombing of the *Lancastria* despite the presence of No. 1 Squadron's *Hurricanes* made a deep impression.[15]

By the morning of June 18th their task was almost complete. A few more sorties had yet to be flown; McKnight recorded a two hour escort flight with a reconnaissance aircraft, and Grassick flew a 90 minute patrol over St. Nazaire. Meanwhile the destruction of supplies continued. Three or four unserviceable *Hurricanes* were burned.[16] There was some question about how to set the fuel stocks on fire; prudence dictated that they be left alone rather than risk self-immolation. At last they were ready; at 11:00 a.m. ten of No. 242's airworthy fighters took off, heading for England.

They had been airborne about half an hour, having overflown the *Hurricane* Stansfeld had "pranged" a few days previously. It was still there. Abruptly, Gobeil whipped over into a dive, followed by Stansfeld. The others did not follow this unexpected manoeuvre; it was the last glimpse most of them ever had of their Commanding Officer.

Stansfeld did not know what had led Gobeil to break away from the others. Then he saw the reason—a lone *He 111* bomber further down. Gobeil was going too fast and overshot the target. Stansfeld opened fire, shot it down, then reformed with his leader. Separated from the others, they carried on to Christchurch, on the south coast of England, where they put down with their fuel exhausted. In the confusion of the homecoming, Stansfeld failed to submit a Combat Report; the only known record of the engagement with the Heinkel is his logbook entry. This also indicates the lengths

on the cockpit lights betraying the presence of the base to the Germans. It is difficult to imagine that the dim reddish glow of such lights could reveal anything to an aircraft several thousand feet up. See Stan Turner, "Over France", *The Canadians at War 1939-45* (Montreal, 1969), Volume 1, p. 40.

15. No. 73 Squadron's ORB mentions no sightings of enemy aircraft, while Grassick, Crowley-Milling, McKnight, and Stansfeld record no action—negative evidence, admittedly, that *Luftwaffe* raids were sporadic. Nantes at this time was probably outside the range of *Ju 87* and *Bf 109* aircraft.

16. James J. Halley's studies of RAF aircraft in the L-, N-, and P- series record that No. 242's N2381, P3683, and P3779 were burned at Nantes. L1757 was also destroyed; it may not have been on the strength of No. 242 at that time.

to which a *Hurricane* could be pushed—he recorded being airborne two hours and 50 minutes!

Pilot Officers Grassick and Campbell and Sergeant Richardson had been overlooked. They left about 30 minutes after their comrades, having difficulty in starting their engines without groundcrew. Taking off without maps or clear orders about where to land, they ran out of fuel and force-landed in the area of Dunster Beach, between Watchet and Minehead. The remaining pilots (Atkinson, Bush, Crowley-Milling, Eckford, Latta, McKnight, Plinston, and Turner) completed a two hour and 30 minute flight directly from Nantes to Tangmere. After refuelling they proceeded to Coltishall.[17]

Whether such an endurance test was necessary is open to question. The route taken had brought them near Jersey, and one may ask why an intermediate stop was not scheduled there. That island was still in British hands, No. 17 Squadron was still flying its *Hurricanes* from there to cover the last evacuations from Cherbourg. In retrospect it must be concluded that some lives and aircraft were endangered by making the direct flight from Nantes to England.

Pilot Officer Neil Campbell later wrote a remarkable letter to his mother, describing No. 242's experiences in France. One is left to wonder how it ever got past a censor, for it included much classified information. His narrative is worth quoting in full:

> We didn't lose many men while we were in France—one is missing and one is in hospital suffering from nerves. We had a rather good tour in France. We were based at Nantes, Le Mans, Chateauduex [sic] sometimes operating from a forward base. One was near Remouley. It was quite a forward base.
>
> We covered the evacuation from Nantes and prevented it from becoming another Dunkirk. There were about three squadrons at Nantes covering the troopships and with pardonable pride we kept "Jerry" off. One evening the wily devil sent over five Heinkels. They came over high and approached from different directions. One succeeded in diving through the clouds and bombed one of our ships but that couldn't be helped. They glided down from a height and dived through the clouds. Unfortunately the first bomb

17. Pilot Officer Horne, a replacement pilot, had been posted to No. 32 Squadron on June 12th; all pilots who had gone to France were thus accounted for.

got the ship, No. 1 Squadron. The squadron was on patrol at the time and succeeded in shooting down three of the Huns. One was chased, not shot, into the water. Boy, he must have been scared.

We serviced our aircraft for about three or four days in order to allow our troops to get on the transports. It certainly was hard work. Up at 3.15 o'clock in the morning, at readiness at 4.00 a.m., on patrol at 5.30 o'clock until 7.00 o'clock; then we had to refuel our own aircraft after we landed. We finished work about ten in the evening. So you see I can work when it is necessary, but I certainly was tired. Just a case of rolling into bed and rolling out in the morning.

When we started for England we had no maps, so we didn't end up where we should have. Our section, Bob Grassick of London, Ont., Sergeant Richardson, and myself landed on the beach at Minehead in Somerset. We were unfortunate—or fortunate—enough to run out of petrol at this point. It is really a wizard of a place, quite as nice as anything I have seen. The people were very nice. They actually pushed my machine up a 200 foot hill that had a one-third rise. The last three feet were perpendicular so my machine literally had to be lifted up. Landing on the beach tipped up the nose of my plane, breaking the airscrew. Bob tore his tailwheel and rudder; Sergeant Richardson tore off his tail wheel, fairing and rudder, and also went up on his nose.

It was rather disappointing for it was my first "all my own" machine—a brand new "Rotal" Hurricane, P2985 "N". With the letter and all you can see why I was sorry to lose it; but I am getting another new machine. It arrived today and is going to be "S" for St. Thomas. I am going to steal Leslie Charteris' "Saint", as an emblem and under it I hope to put "Tom". So I will be flying in St. Thomas. Bob Grassick has "L" for London.[18]

18. Undated and unidentified newspaper clipping in Grassick scrapbook. Rotol constant speed propellers had been fitted to the *Hurricanes* in early June, replacing the two-position propellers of earlier models. The choice of a landing site was odd, in that the three pilots had flown over much of South-Western England before coming down on the south shore of the Bristol Channel. Campbell's "Saint" insignia did not materialize; it was used by another pilot months later.

How many victories the Canadians achieved during the June campaign cannot be determined with certainty. The squadron records are vague, and no Combat Reports have come down to us. The best information available consists of logbook entries by a few pilots, together with newspaper accounts of questionable accuracy. It would appear, however, that McKnight, Stansfeld, and Turner each destroyed two enemy aircraft; the squadron total was possibly higher.[19] One pilot, MacQueen, had been lost in action.

And so No. 242 Squadron came home. It was battered and the men were tired; Stansfeld would write home that "bad weather now is when the sun is shining, and good weather when the clouds are down to the ground."[20] The unit's Canadian blood was being thinned as British pilots had begun to replace Canadians. None of this was apparent to the folks back in Canada. Newspapers there printed sporadic reports of pilots "missing" (often with the expressed hope of their survival), trumpeted the news of Willie McKnight's Distinguished Flying Cross, and printed grossly inaccurate estimates of No. 242's victories.[21]

The prevailing mood among No. 242's members was one of frustration. In part this stemmed from bewilderment at their being sent to the Continent when the situation was beyond recovery. Similar views were held by Canadian soldiers who had been despatched to France, only to turn about and evacuate before the enemy could be engaged.[22] In retrospect it is clear that there was no hope of maintaining a foothold in France, but this was not so obvious when the decision had been taken to make that attempt. The speedy collapse of France had surprised both her ally and enemy, neither of whom fully appreciated how ill-organized her forces had been.

19. McKnight's generally accepted wartime "score" (and one cited by this author in *The Tumbling Sky*) is 16½ enemy aircraft destroyed. In view of his logbook entry for June 14th (presumably checked by his Commanding Officer), this total might well be raised to 18½.

20. "Vancouver Flier Has Bag of Six German Warplanes", Vancouver *Sun*, July 19th, 1940.

21. A terrible example of this "puffery" is provided by Allen Bill, "Canadian Pilots Victors, 101 to 16", Edmonton *Journal*, June 19th, 1940.

22. See C.P. Stacey, *Six Years of War*, (Ottawa, 1955), pp. 279-285.

The pilots in particular were angry with all authority (both Turner and Crowley-Milling described their sentiments as being "Bolshi"), but whether such attitudes were justifiable can be debated.

The end of the campaign in France also marked the conclusion of Squadron Leader Gobeil's tenure as Commanding Officer of No. 242. He did not rejoin the pilots at Coltishall; instead he was attached to RCAF Overseas Headquarters and returned to Canada in mid-July.[23] The manner of his going has never been satisfactorily explained, although two writers have hinted that there was somehow a failure in leadership on his part.[24]

Gobeil's actions may be criticised on some points. On May 23rd and June 18th he had broken formation to attack enemy aircraft, which may indicate some lack of personal air discipline. His decision to send the groundcrew from Chateaudun without an officer to assume responsibility might be open to question, though it may well have been dictated by the shortage of such officers. The unexpected departure of those groundcrew from Nantes on the night of the 15th indicates a lack of communications between Gobeil and MacDonald, on one hand, and the tradesmen on the other. His approach to tactics appears to have been conservative, but this merely reflected the standard doctrines evolved by Fighter Command between the wars.

His contributions should be remembered. It was Gobeil who had lobbied to have No. 242 outfitted as a single-seater fighter squadron. Insofar as his superiors were concerned, he had brought the squadron to an excellent level of performance before it was declared operational; this opinion was confirmed when No. 242 was selected to serve in France in June 1940. The heavy casualties sustained in May were a factor of intense operations; the losses among detached squadron personnel on the Continent in May were not attributable to the condition of No. 242, but to the state of Nos. 85, 607, and 615 Squadrons, to which they had been attached. In June

23. Squadron Leader Gobeil took up instructional duties with the British Commonwealth Air Training Plan. In 1943 he was awarded the Air Force Cross for his participation in a dangerous experiment—the towing of a *CG-4* glider in stages across the Atlantic. He remained in the RCAF after the war, attaining the rank of Wing Commander in 1948 and retiring in 1956.

24. See Turner, note 14, and Paul Brickhill, *Reach for the Sky* (London, 1954), p. 183.

the squadron was successfully extricated from a situation where further operations would have been meaningless, though amid considerable confusion.

No. 242's first Commanding Officer would suffer by comparison with his successor, Douglas Bader, one of the RAF's outstanding leaders and personalities. The full story of Squadron Leader Gobeil's departure has not yet been told, and will have to wait for a study by historians with more access to confidential documents than was available to this writer. Until then, the mixed opinions of his performance in command of No. 242 Squadron must be set against his subsequent creditable record.

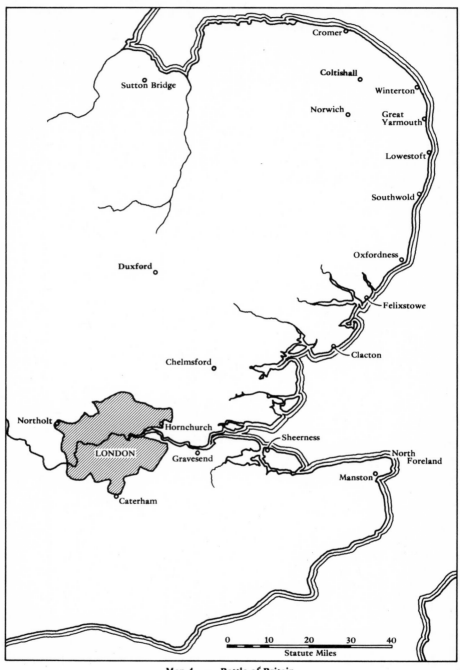

Map 4 - Battle of Britain

Battle of Britain

On June 24th Squadron Leader D.R.S. Bader took command of No. 242 at Coltishall, where the unit had begun to take shape again. Bader was one of the most incredible men in the RAF, combining courage, charm, rudeness, and humanity in one awesome package. Both his legs had been amputated following a crash in 1931, and he had been released from the RAF. When war broke out Bader succeeded in convincing his superiors that he was fit to fly. Once back in the air force he proceeded to impress all with his cockpit skills and leadership.

Men who served under Bader soon forgot his handicap and were swept up in his enthusiasm for life. He played golf and squash, socialized freely, talked "shop" constantly, and always at a pace that left others gasping. Having overcome a fearful disability, he used his experiences to help others. One pilot witnessed a moving instance of this; he and Bader had stopped (at Bader's insistence) at a London hospital. They went to a children's ward, where Bader was introduced as "the pilot with no legs". The young patients protested that he clearly had legs, and Bader removed his trousers to display his artificial limbs. He then took these off and walked on his hands for the length of the ward and back. As he conducted this performance for the delighted children, a nurse remarked to the junior pilot, "Every time he comes here, he does more good than a dozen therapists."[1]

Late June brought a swarm of new pilots—Flight Lieutenant G.E. Ball (who replaced Miller as commander of "A" Flight), and Sergeants J.F. Armitage, G.W. Brimble, A.D. Meredith, J.A. Porter, and Terras (initials unknown). All, like Bader, were British. The Canadian nature of the squadron was somewhat restored in July with the return of Pilot Officers Benzie and Brown, who had been wounded in May, and with the posting in of Pilot Officer Norris Hart on July 18th. Born in Montreal but raised in Hamilton, Hart was a cheerful, witty man whose commission dated only from July 7th. He was immediately sent to No. 5 Operational Training Unit, Aston Down, for advanced instruction, and reported back to the squadron on August 12th.

Hart was followed by Flying Officer George Patterson Christie of Westmount, Quebec, who came to No. 242 on July 21st. Christie, a member of the RAF since 1937, had a remarkable operational record. For the first seven months of the war he had flown *Hurricanes* with No. 43 Squadron. In June of 1940 he had joined the Photo Development Unit, Heston, which was working out the techniques of modern photographic reconnaissance using unarmed, high-altitude *Spitfires*. His pioneering work would be recognized with the award of a Distinguished Flying Cross in August 1940.

If Canadians still arrived, however, so too did more British pilots. Flight Lieutenant G.F. Powell-Sheddon, a man with a Cranwell background and a pronounced stutter, succeeded Plinston as "B" Flight Commander early in July.[2] Pilots from the Royal Navy's Fleet Air Arm were being lent to the RAF in the summer of 1940

1. Interview with C.I.R. Arthur, November 21st, 1980.

2. See Paul Brickhill, *Reach for the Sky* (London, 1954), pp. 183-184. In describing Bader's re-organization of the squadron, Brickhill sometimes omits names, but he suggests that Plinston was either deemed unsuitable (for unspecified reasons) or was pining for a non-operational posting. It should be remembered that this officer had come to No. 242 with a satisfactory record, and had done good work over Dunkirk. Later in the war he would win a Distinguished Flying Cross, having shot down seven enemy aircraft while serving with Nos. 607, 242, 3 (RAAF), and 250 Squadrons; he commanded No. 601 Squadron briefly in March 1943.

to help fill the gaps in Fighter Command's ranks for the battle that was obviously impending. Three were posted to No. 242 on July 1st, Sub-Lieutenants R.J. Cork and R.E. Gardner and Midshipman R.J. Patterson, and on July 20th Sergeant R.V. Lonsdale arrived.

The "de-Canadianization" of No. 242 was apparent in other ways. With the departure of Squadron Leader Gobeil the last formal link with the RCAF was severed; Bader certainly did not report on the squadron to Canadian authorities and may have been completely unaware of the unit's original purpose—to be a quasi-official Canadian presence and possibly to become an RCAF formation. Visits from assorted Canadian senior officers and dignitaries ceased. Why this happened is uncertain. There is no evidence either that they were discouraged from coming (as an RAF officer like Bader, intent on getting the unit battle-ready again, might have done) or that the Canadian "brass" had lost interest (which might well have happened, as by the summer of 1940 there were three RCAF squadrons in Britain to absorb the attention of Canadian officialdom).

In fact, it became apparent that No. 242 Squadron, as a Canadian unit, to which this country owed some responsibility, had never been fully understood by the Canadian government. Senior RCAF officers and various Canadian High Commission Staff, from Vincent Massey down, had kept a paternal watch on the outfit, but the political leaders clearly had not thought out the implications of advocating a "Canadian" squadron in the RAF. It attracted scant official comment; throughout its history No. 242 Squadron was mentioned only once in the Canadian House of Commons. On July 29th, 1940 the Honourable C.G. Power (Minister for Air) was speaking in general terms about the war effort. He mentioned the Canadians who had enlisted directly in the RAF, then went on to say:

> A large number of these have been formed into a Canadian squadron in the Royal Air Force. This squadron has already been in contact with the enemy. Unfortunately there have been many casualties, but we learn with some degree of pride from the ever-lengthening lists of awards and decorations that these young men now in the Royal Air Force bid fair to emulate those who twenty years ago brought honour and glory to the name of Canada.[3]

3. *House of Commons Debates*, July 29th, 1940, p. 2104.

It was fine rhetoric, but the statement suggested that "Chubby" Power had only the vaguest idea about No. 242 Squadron. No member of the House questioned him about the casualties, or Canadian replacements to be supplied. The press still wrote of an "all-Canadian squadron in the Royal Air Force", assuming that Canada was administering it in some way. Hanson Baldwin, military expert for the New York *Times*, would declare that the RCAF was "maintaining four squadrons overseas—one R.A.F. all-Canadian fighter squadron, one Royal Canadian Air Force fighter squadron, and two army co-operation squadrons".[4] In fact, No. 242 was a RAF unit, pure and simple; by freak circumstances attending its birth it happened to have a substantially higher proportion of Canadians than other RAF units at that time. The only Canadian holding a position of any responsibility in the unit was Flying Officer MacDonald, the adjutant.

Some days elapsed during which Squadron Leader Bader and his new Flight Commanders adjusted to the veteran pilots, and the incoming flying personnel were absorbed. The Commanding Officer and his staff also had to secure the spare parts, tools, and ground servicing equipment that were vital for keeping the aircraft in flying, fighting trim. Even the most basic tools had been lost or left behind in the retreat from France. Once these supplies had arrived, and with the help of perfect flying weather, No. 242 settled into intensive training.

Not only did the pilots have to be knit into a new team, but lessons learned in France had to be incorporated—tactics, the proper means of gun harmonization, and the problems of keeping station in battle situations. On July 6th, during air firing practice at No. 6 OTU's range at Sutton Bridge, the pilots achieved scores that were a record for Fighter Command to that date; Pilot Officer Stansfeld had the highest number of hits in the squadron.[5]

4. Hanson Baldwin, "As Others See Us", Winnipeg *Free Press*, October 8th, 1940.

5. Brickhill, *op.cit.*, paints a picture of a sullen, near-mutinous squadron, suffering from low morale until Bader arrived to inspire the men, clean house, and bully the RAF bureaucracy into issuing the necessary stores. One wonders whether, if No. 242 was in such bad shape as Brickhill suggests, it could have achieved such splendid results so soon. It should be recalled that No. 242 had

In essence the tactics being rehearsed remained those developed by the pre-war RAF, based on sections of three aircraft flying in V-formation (vics). The French campaign had demonstrated the merits of German methods, which employed loose four-plane and two-plane units with great flexibility. Nevertheless, there was no time to re-write the manual, retrain veteran pilots, and indoctrinate the tyros. The RAF vics were widened, and two or three "weavers" were assigned to protect the tails of the squadrons. These innovations improved the effectiveness of the *Hurricanes* and *Spitfires*, though *Luftwaffe* tactical formations remained superior. Not until the winter of 1940-41 would Fighter Command be able to copy wholesale the "finger-four" pattern employed by the enemy. Fighter Command was also slow to adopt a simple but dramatically effective modification, wherein the guns were harmonized so that their fire converged about 120 yards ahead of the aircraft, rather than the standard 400 yards. Pilots were not encouraged to attack from close quarters; instead they were still told to fire at ranges where deadly effects were achieved as much by good luck as good management.[6]

At mid-day on July 9th the squadron was again declared operational, having been out of the line for three weeks. First blood in the new period was drawn the morning of the 10th, when No. 242 was assigned to patrol over a convoy sailing down the Norfolk coast. Several *He 111* bombers appeared, and ships' anti-aircraft fire led the *Hurricanes* directly to the enemy. Pilot Officer Eckford chased one through clouds, shot at it, and disabled the rear gunner before exhausting his own ammunition. Sub-Lieutenant Gardner attacked another *He 111* that was attempting to bomb the convoy. After

turned in a fine performance when it had been examined and declared operational the previous March. Obviously, somebody had to be doing *something* right before Bader arrived. Moreover, Bader seems to have packed clout and influence far exceeding his rank. In part this could be attributed to his dynamic personality, but other factors must be mentioned. As a graduate of the Royal Air Force College, Cranwell, he could tap the RAF's "old boy network". Len Deighton has suggested another factor—the influence of MacDonald, the MP Adjutant with upper class connections, who probably used his own influence on Bader's behalf. See Len Deighton, *Fighter: The True Story of the Battle of Britain* (London, 1977), p. 229.

6. See Alfred Price, *Battle of Britain: The Hardest Day: 18 August 1940* (Macdonald and Jane's, London, 1979) pp. 27-28 and 41-43.

three firing passes by Gardner, the Heinkel, belonging to III/KG 53, crashed into the Channel and sank; one crewman was seen to emerge onto the wing. In a later patrol Pilot Officer Latta pressed home an attack on yet another *He 111*, whose rear gunner put a bullet through the Canadian's wing. The bomber escaped into cloud at 4,000 feet, its starboard engine smoking.[7]

The following morning, July 11th, Squadron Leader Bader was flying a dawn patrol near Cromer. About 6:10 a.m. he intercepted a *Do 17* flying at 1,000 feet. Bader fired two long bursts that consumed all his ammunition. He was unable to observe the effects of his attack owing to rain and low cloud, into which the Dornier had plunged. The Royal Observer Corps, however, confirmed that the bomber had crashed into the sea.

These actions, coming so swiftly, raised hopes of more to follow, but the balance of the month was passed with base patrols, convoy patrols, and futile scrambles after unseen intruders. The only additional success came on the morning of July 23rd, when Flight Lieutenant Powell-Sheddon destroyed a *Ju 88* southeast of Yarmouth.[8]

Convoy patrols were necessary, as long as the British continued to run ships down a coast exposed to enemy air raids, but one could not protect everything at once. In the mid-afternoon of August 1st, while Nos. 66 and 242 Squadrons were preoccupied with a convoy, the *Luftwaffe* bombed nearby Norwich and escaped without losses. Retribution followed in the early evening.

Flying Officer Christie had taken off at 5:47 p.m., accompanied by Pilot Officer Latta and Sergeant Richardson. Their task was to protect a convoy sailing past Lowestoft. A solid layer extended from 1,000 to 2,000 feet; below that visibility was six miles in haze. As they approached their charges the *Hurricane* pilots saw anti-

7. Latta's Combat Report was filed with No. 242 Squadron's Operational Record Book Appendices, but not with Air Ministry. Some details of these and other Battle of Britain combats have been extracted from Francis K. Mason, *Battle Over Britain* (London, 1969), an excellent day-by-day account of the campaign. His compilation of German unit losses is particularly impressive.

8. This action is listed by Mason, *op.cit*, p. 188, but is not mentioned in Wing Commander Hitchins' original narrative. It is also omitted from Chris Shores' *Aces High* (London, 1966).

aircraft shells bursting. The smoke puffs led them to the attacking aircraft, a mixed bag of *Ju 88's* and *He 111's*.

The bombers kept popping in and out of cloud, never visible for more than a few seconds before vanishing into the murk again. The fighter pilots played a game of tag with the enemy, who would appear, drop a bomb, then duck into the cloud again. The attack was unco-ordinated as the enemy appeared singly, their bomb loads scattered across the sea, not even near the ships.

The *Hurricanes* split up to drive off the Germans. Latta attacked three different aircraft, snapping off two-second bursts at long range, all to no effect. Christie engaged a series of *He 111's*, pursuing one for some miles over the Channel before returning to the ships. About 6:50 p.m. a bomber dropped out of the clouds and into his gunsight. Christie fired and gave chase as it climbed through the clouds. Only his own shortage of fuel forced him to break off the action. He was credited with the probable destruction of an *He 111*; he had, in fact, shot up a *Ju 88* of 2/KG 30, killing two crewmen and wounding a third. The bomber force-landed in Denmark. Sergeant Richardson shot down a *Ju 88* of 9/KG 4 about the same time.

The small number of interceptions reflected the fact that No. 242 Squadron was stationed away from the centre of action. Things were different over the southern and southeastern counties of England. Intense skirmishing had been in progress since the beginning of July—the opening rounds of the Battle of Britain.

The dates of that battle are generally cited as July 10th to October 31st, 1940; aircrew who flew operational sorties in designated *fighter* squadrons between these two dates were later issued with a Battle of Britain Clasp to their 1939-1945 Star. In retrospect we can see that the *real* Battle of Britain was of much shorter duration. The importance of the campaign lay in this question: who would control British airspace in any area selected for a German invasion? Hitler's Directive No. 16, authorizing planning for an invasion, was not issued until July 16th. *Adlertag*, the kickoff to the *Luftwaffe* assault on the RAF, was scheduled for August 10th, scratched by weather, and not launched in full earnest until the 13th. The Battle of Britain then went through two distinct phases— the German attack on RAF fields, sector stations, and radar posts (lasting until September 6th), succeeded by large daylight raids on London. In this latter phase the Germans handicapped themselves by committing bombers to a target at the limit of *Bf 109* fighter cover. *Seelöwe* (the planned invasion itself), having been put off twice, was postponed indefinitely on September 17th because the *Luftwaffe* could not guarantee secure air space over the proposed landing areas. German air operations thereafter lacked the strategic implications of those between August 13th and September 16th.

Coltishall, an airfield controlled by No. 12 Group, was on the northern flank of the primary battle area, and action was correspondingly sporadic. On August 19th enemy aircraft raided the field. Five bombs exploded near a hangar, killing two men and causing slight damage to the building itself. Eight *Hurricanes* took off to patrol the base but were too late to catch the bombers.

Low cloud covered the aerodrome the following day and six aircraft patrolled over their base to guard against another enemy attack. During the patrol Midshipman Patterson in P2976 spun and crashed in the sea five miles northeast of Winterton. He was killed; the cause of the crash was unknown.

Following a series of large air battles in the south and north, the *Luftwaffe* took advantage of a period of bad weather to relax. Fighter Command was not permitted the same luxury. On August 21st, when cloud and occasional rain prevailed over England, the Germans despatched a series of small raiding forces, none larger than three aircraft. No. 242 got no rest; the unit flew 29 sorties between 8:40 a.m. and 2:15 p.m.

Blue Section, led by Powell-Sheddon, was scrambled at noon to patrol Norwich. Over that city they were instructed to steer 190 degrees (almost due south). They were on that course when they sighted a *Do 17* flying at 3,500 feet between two layers of cloud.

Powell-Sheddon gave it a squirt before it reached the lower blanket of cloud. The Dornier went right through with three *Hurricanes* snapping at it. Pilot Officer Latta (Blue 2) found himself underneath the bomber and about 100 yards away. He allowed 25 degrees deflection and gave it a six-second burst. Simultaneously Blue 3 (Sub-Lieutenant Gardner) carried out an attack. There was no return fire. The Dornier's port engine began to burn, and there seemed to be a fire in its fuselage as well. The pilot attempted to land but crashed in a wood. The *Do 17*, from 4/KG 3, burst into flames.[9]

9. CAN/RAF cards compiled by Wing Commander Hitchins indicate a three-

Squadron Leader Bader, flying a lone patrol, also encountered a *Do 17* that day. After one firing pass he lost it in clouds. The encounter seemed inconclusive at the time; in his logbook he wrote, "Hit it but saw no result". Later, on the basis of bodies washed ashore whose documents and stopped watches linked them with the Dornier, Bader was credited with a victory.[10]

There were still comings and goings as personnel were posted to and from No. 242, reflecting both its needs and those of other units. Out went Sergeant Armitage (posted at an indeterminate date in August), Sergeant Meredith (sent to No. 141 Squadron on August 9th), Sergeant Porter (transferred on the 10th to No. 615 Squadron), Pilot Officer Atkinson (posted to No. 600 Squadron, also on the 10th), and Pilot Officer Waterton (posted to No. 6 Operational Training Unit on the 20th). The last-named officer had been inactive since his crash in May.[11]

Four Canadian pilots, each with different backgrounds and experiences, were posted in to No. 242. The first to arrive was Pilot Officer Hugh Norman Tamblyn of Watrous and North Battleford, Saskatchewan, who reported on August 5th. Tall and strikingly handsome, he was also noted for his optimistic yet taciturn nature. He had learned to fly while working as an aircraft mechanic in Saskatoon. Tamblyn had obtained his Short Service Commission on June 4th, 1938; he came to No. 242 after a short but harrowing tour with No. 141 Squadron flying *Defiants*. He was followed by Flying Officer John Geoffrey Cave, British-born but educated in Calgary (1927-32) where he later worked (1934-35). Cave had been in the RAF since January 1939. He had already flown with No. 600

way division of credit; the Combat Report with a notation by an Intelligence Officer divides it between Latta and Gardner; Mason, *op.cit.*, and Shores, *op.cit.*, give the victory to Gardner alone.

10. Not mentioned in Mason, *op.cit.*, but referred to in Brickhill, *Reach for the Sky*, pp. 199-201, and in *The All Canadian Squadron*. Brickhill indicates that upgrading of the action to a "destroyed" came within days of the encounter; Hitchins states that confirmation of the victory did not come through until December 28th, 1940.

11. Waterton became an instructor, then went on to be a test pilot. He was awarded the Air Force Cross (January 1st, 1943), Bar to the AFC (June 12th, 1947), and George Medal (July 29th, 1952).

Squadron, but does not appear to have taken part in any operations with No. 242; his assignment may have been temporary pending another posting.

Next in was Pilot Officer Kirkpatrick Maclure Sclanders, who reported on August 26th. Born in Saskatoon and raised in Saint John, New Brunswick, the 25-year old pilot had learned to fly at the age of 15, but had been forced to wait until his 17th birthday before he could be tested for his Private Pilot's License. Boyish in appearance, he had become a familiar figure at Maritime air shows where he dressed as a boy scout, climbed into a light aircraft, "accidentally" started the engine, took off, and then performed several sloppy aerobatics while spectators gasped at the thought of an utterly untrained lad floundering in the cockpit. In September 1935 Sclanders had joined the RAF, and later flew with No. 25 (Fighter) Squadron. In the summer of 1937 he had resigned his commission due to ill-health, returned to Canada, and taken up journalism. Surgery had restored him to flying trim, yet the RCAF refused to accept him. When the Russo-Finnish War broke out, Sclanders volunteered for that, only to be disappointed by the war's end. By this time it was the spring of 1940. He applied to join the French Air Force. That country collapsed before he could act; he escaped from Southern France with a boatload of Polish refugees. The RAF now took him back, commissioning him once more on July 25th. He was given a hurried course in flying monoplanes, then despatched to No. 242 Squadron.[12]

The last of the new boys was Pilot Officer Lawrence Elwood Cryderman, a thoughtful school-teacher from Toronto who reported to No. 242 on August 31st. He had been in the RAF since March 1939. Cryderman would be a social asset to the squadron by virtue of his skill as a pianist; it was said that he "could do anything with a piano except prang it".[13] Unfortunately, he lacked fighter experience. He was promptly packed off to No. 5 Operational Training Unit on September 5th and did not return to the squadron until the 26th.

Convoy patrols had, as usual, taken up most of No. 242's time

12. Saint John *Telegraph-Journal*, September 12th, 1940.

13. R.H. Dibnah to the author, November 20th, 1980.

during the last few days of August. The only untoward incident had been on the ground, where "Slim" Grassick sustained injuries in a motorcycle accident that would keep him out of action for a month.

On the morning of the 30th the squadron was ordered from Coltishall to Duxford, much nearer London. This was not a whole-sale movement; No. 242 would thereafter regularly fly to Duxford in the morning and back to Coltishall each evening. It was not until the week of October 19th-26th that Duxford was made "home base" for No. 242.

What mattered was that, with the Battle of Britain raging toward its climax, the pilots were now closer to the main event. They realized the implications; for days they had followed the course of the campaign through the papers, radio, and RAF intelligence summaries. On that first, fair day, winging down to Duxford, there was keen anticipation and knotted nerves among them.

In the late afternoon the squadron was abruptly scrambled to meet an incoming raid which seemed to threaten North Weald aerodrome. In an effort to get the advantage of the sun, Bader ignored the instructions of a ground controller and turned west momentarily to have the sun behind him. Three *Hurricanes* were detached to investigate some suspicious aircraft, leaving eleven fighters. They were over North Weald when Flying Officer Christie drew the attention of his comrades to a "vast number" of twin-engined enemy aircraft—*Bf 110's* plus bombers—flying east. One group of 70 or 80 was at 12-14,000 feet, with another swarm stepped up above that at 15-20,000 feet. No other British fighters seemed to be about.

Bader ordered Christie's section to tackle the upper layer of aircraft. He then dived straight into the middle of the tightly-packed enemy formation with the object of breaking it up and starting a dogfight; the other fighters streamed in behind him, trying to approximate a line-astern formation. Bader's "bull-in-a-chinashop" tactic succeeded admirably. The Messerschmitts scattered fanwise and the *Hurricanes* were soon in business. Bader saw three *'110's* break right and three more break left in front of him. Following one group, he fired at point-blank range into one and saw it disintegrate in a mass of flames. He immediately engaged another *Bf 110*, carried out two attacks, and saw it go down burning in a spiral dive. He narrowly escaped an aggressive *'110*, then suddenly found himself alone in the sky.

Bader's two wingmen, McKnight and Crowley-Milling, enjoyed

equally good hunting. Crowley-Milling pounced on an *He 111* that had broken from its formation. He had trouble with a determined German gunner, but managed to silence the man and set the Heinkel's starboard engine smoking before a *Bf 110* drove him off. He did not see the bomber crash, but Norris Hart reported seeing it descending in flames, so a "destroyed" claim was recorded.

It was McKnight who had the most spectacular success that day. His Combat Report vividly describes the encounter:

> While patrolling with squadron over North Weald enemy sighted on left at 1705 (approx.) enemy a/c in vic formation stepped from 12,000-18,000 ft., attacked middle section of '110s and two enemy a/c broke off to attack. Succeeded in getting behind one enemy and opened fire at approx. 100 yds; enemy a/c burst into flames and dived towards ground. Next attacked He.111 formation and carried out beam attack on nearest one opening fire at approx. 150-200 yards. Port engine stopped and a/c rolled over on back, finally starting to smoke then burst into flames and crashed to earth. Lastly was attacked by Me.110 but succeeded in getting behind and followed him from 10,000 ft to 1,000 ft. Enemy a/c used very steep turns for evasive action but finally straightened out. I opened fire at approx. 30 yards, enemy's starboard engine stopped and port engine burst into flames. Enemy crashed in flames alongside large reservoir. No rear fire noticed from first two enemy but last machine used large amount.

While Bader's Red Section was winning its six victories, climaxed by McKnight's "hat trick", Yellow Section (Flight Lieutenant Ball, Sub-Lieutenant Cork, Sergeant Lonsdale) was shooting down two *He 111's* and one *Bf 110*, plus two *'110's* probably destroyed.[14] Green Section, led by Flying Officer Christie, meanwhile tackled the top layer of enemy aircraft, breaking their formation. Christie attacked a *Bf 110* head on—a very dangerous tactic because the *'110* packed a heavy wallop of firepower in its nose. The German broke to starboard and went into a dive with the *Hurri-*

14. Hitchins, *The All Canadian Squadron*, writes that Yellow Section scored three destroyed, one probable, and one damaged. Intelligence Reports supplied to this author by the RAF Museum list the following: one *He 111* destroyed by Ball (shared wth Stansfeld), one *Bf 110* probably destroyed by Ball, one *Bf 110* destroyed and one *Bf 110* probably destroyed by Cork, one *He 111* destroyed by Lonsdale.

cane following. Christie made certain that nobody was after him, then began delivering successive bursts from a range of 50 yards. Oil began spurting from the starboard engine, after which the enemy's fuel tank exploded. From 6,000 feet the *Bf 110* went into a vertical dive, crashing in a greenhouse near Ponders' End.[15]

Pilot Officer Hart (Green 3) dived on three *He 111's* that were flying in line-astern formation while being harried by Crowley-Milling and Ball. The Canadian selected one which then went into a dive. Rather than follow it, he turned inside another Heinkel and gave it everything. The bomber went down in flames and crashed in a field, killing the entire crew. The Heinkel was from 5/KG 1. Hart then broke away to escape three very angry Messerschmitts.

Black Section—two *Hurricanes* flown by Pilot Officer Stansfeld and Sergeant Brimble—had covered the rear of the squadron during the initial attack on the German formations. Brimble shot down a *Bf 110* in flames, then mauled another in a head-on pass in which he was certain he killed the enemy pilot; it was credited to him as a "probable".

Stansfeld sighted a straggling *He 111* going east and went after it, delivering three attacks with Flight Lieutenant Ball assisting. As he made his first firing pass he saw the rear gun winking "like a flashlight going on and off". He put the gunner out of action, then set the port engine smoking. The starboard engine simply stopped, and the bomber crashed on a civil airfield covered with wrecked cars (presumably to prevent its possible use by German airborne troops).[16]

It had been a terrific fight, with twelve confirmed "kills" credited to various pilots, and not one of the *Hurricanes* damaged. Back at base the pilots trooped to the squadron Intelligence Officer to recount their experiences, trying to compress the frenetic dog-

15. Christie was posted to No. 66 Squadron on September 3rd. Later he was promoted to Squadron Leader and posted to Canada, only to die in an air accident on July 6th, 1942.

16. The Squadron Operational Record Book gives the battle as an early afternoon affair, but the Combat Reports and intelligence summaries agree that takeoff was at 4:23 or 4:26 p.m., combat at 5:00-5:05 p.m., and touchdown at 5:35 p.m. Brickhill, *op.cit.*, pp. 204-206, mentions that Crowley-Milling first reported the enemy formation, but intelligence summaries single Christie out for this. The book also credits Turner with a victory; this is an error, for Turner did not fly that day.

fights into the cold prose of official Combat Reports. A reporter on hand noted their casual air; it seemed as though supper rather than the air battle was the most important thing on their minds. Of Willie McKnight it was noted that he "whistled quietly as he sat beside the intelligence officer completing the form and looking for all the world like a high school boy doing homework".[17]

Congratulations poured in. The Chief of the Air Staff signalled, "Magnificent fighting. You are well on top of the enemy and obviously the fine Canadian traditions of the last war are safe in your hands." The Under-Secretary of State for Air and the Air Officer Commanding, No. 12 Group (Air Vice Marshal Trafford Leigh-Mallory) added their congratulations "on a first class show". Significantly, there were no telegrams from Canadian officials, neither civil nor military.[18]

From August 31st to September 6th the squadron continued its patrols over Duxford, Northolt, North Weald, and Hornchurch without making any contact with the enemy. For the period of September 3rd to the 5th they operated from Coltishall; the rest of the time they flew from the forward vantage point of Duxford. Although the pilots saw no German aircraft, some dramas were played out beyond their sight. On August 31st a force of *Do 17's* and *Bf 110's* slipped through the defences and headed for Duxford when none of the squadrons there were at an advanced state of readiness. Fortunately, Wing Commander A. Woodhall, the senior controller, was able to direct nine *Hurricanes* of No. 111 Squadron to meet the enemy head-on and smash the raid before it got under-way.[19]

The *Luftwaffe* had so far been concentrating mainly upon RAF airfields in southern and southeastern England—the area where

17. Undated, unidentified clipping, Grassick scrapbook.

18. Readers should remember that RAF claims and "credits" frequently exceeded the number of enemy aircraft actually destroyed—a problem shared with other air forces. In the case of the battle of August 30th, it seems probable that in the confusion some "double counting" occurred. Even with the best wills involved, the assessment of actions and claims was an inexact science. For a more thorough discussion of this matter see the author's *The Tumbling Sky*, pp. 2-3.

19. Mason, *op.cit*, p. 328.

air superiority would be vital as that was the proposed region for the *Seelöwe* landings. Nevertheless, a series of events had been taking place that would divert the enemy from a campaign they had been on the verge of winning. On the night of August 24th about one hundred German bombers had raided London itself, aiming at no specific targets other than the oil storage depots at Thameshaven. They missed these but started several fires in the city and caused many civilian casualties. The attacks had not been sanctioned by *Reichsmarschall* Göring and led to some recriminations within the German command structure.

More important was the British Cabinet's immediate approval of a reprisal raid upon Berlin, and on the night of August 25th some eighty British bombers operated against the enemy capital. The vicious circle of "retaliation/counter-retaliation" now began on both sides. Believing that Fighter Command was on the ropes, Göring felt confident that he could switch over to a series of punishing raids directed against London. That part of the campaign began on September 7th, and though it meant more hard fighting for the RAF, it also eased pressure on the airfields that had been under ceaseless attack for three weeks. The change in objectives also meant that the *Bf 109* escorts were now operating at the limit of their endurance, with no more than twenty minutes' fuel for battles over London. Göring himself took personal command of the *Luftwaffe* campaign, and his capricious handling of his forces was to sap further their effectiveness. When the definitive histories came to be compiled, virtually all writers would agree that the Germans lost because, lacking a consistent battle plan, they really did not know what they were doing; Fighter Command did.

September 7th began quietly enough, with only a few *Luftwaffe* reconnaissance sorties over England, but in mid-afternoon the enemy threw 348 bombers and 617 fighters into a single massive blow. By 4:17 p.m. Air Vice Marshal Keith Park, Air Officer Commanding No. 11 Group, knew what he was up against and began scrambling every available fighter. The call went out to No. 12 Group for all-out support.

No. 242 had flown from Coltishall to Duxford that morning, joining Nos. 19 and 310 Squadrons (the former a *Spitfire* unit, the latter flying *Hurricanes*). The previous day they had been designated the "Duxford Wing". Shortly before 5:00 p.m. all three squadrons were scrambled to meet the onslaught. They were instructed to patrol North Weald at 10,000 feet but Bader took them to 15,000 feet. As they reached their post anti-aircraft fire directed their attention to enemy aircraft some 5,000 feet above. There were between 70 and 90 of them—bombers in a tight box formation with *Bf 110's* close by and *'109's* higher still. Climbing at full throttle and with maximum boost, No. 242 endeavoured to cut off the raid as quickly as possible.

Within minutes the British fighters were scattered all over the sky. Bader and Cork were the first to reach the enemy. The Commanding Officer set a *Bf 110* on fire before breaking away to escape a yellow-nosed *Bf 109* that had put a bullet through his cockpit. He then engaged another *Bf 110* beneath him and sent it down in flames west of Wickford. Cork also destroyed two of the enemy (a *Do 215* and a *Bf 110*) but had his *Hurricane* considerably damaged by a *Bf 109*. Crowley-Milling shot down another *Bf 110* in flames before he too was attacked from behind by a fighter and forced to crash-land near Chelmsford. Ball destroyed a *Bf 110* in flames; Powell-Sheddon shot down a *Bf 109* that had been attacking a *Hurricane*; Gardner put three bursts into a *Do 215* and saw the crew bale out. Sergeant Lonsdale was credited with a *Do 215* "probably destroyed", while damage claims against *Bf 110's* were submitted by Ball and Bush.

Canadian pilots on this occasion destroyed two enemy aircraft, probably destroyed one, and damaged one more. Pilot Officer Tamblyn went after a *Bf 110*, gave it a five-second burst at 200 yards, then saw it go up in flames. He was beset by a *Bf 109* which he avoided with a steep right-hand turn. That put the *'109* in front of him; he fired for five seconds at 150 yards. The yellow-nosed fighter smoked heavily, dived and climbed a bit, then started down. In the heat of the action Tamblyn was unable to determine its fate; it was credited to him as a "probable". He used the rest of his ammunition firing chance bursts at other aircraft, and regretted having done so when he found himself in a position to "bounce" some straggling *Bf 109's* just when he was out of bullets. He landed at 5:45 p.m., exactly one hour after take-off. The mechanics winced at the sight of his *Hurricane*. It had taken one hit in the port wing and seven in the starboard one.

Pilot Officer Stansfeld singled out what he took to be a *Do 215* which cut loose with a short, inaccurate burst of defensive fire. He began shooting at 300 yards' range from below and to port, and kept pressing the "tit" until he was scarcely 50 yards from his target. The bomber rolled once, started another roll, then dived straight into the ground.[20]

The hectic nature of the action was best illustrated by the experience of Pilot Officer Turner who was leading Green Section, the last *Hurricanes* to join the fray. As he approached the dogfight he saw a *Bf 110* shot down in flames by one of Bader's section. He then fired at a *'110* but before he could press home the attack he had to avoid a *Bf 109*. Turner outmanoeuvred this second opponent, delivered a good burst, and saw the Messerschmitt go into a dive. Another *'109* promptly jumped him. He snapped off a burst at one without visible effect and finally had to take evasive action again. His final score for this action—one *Bf 109* damaged—hardly reflected the fierceness of the dogfight.

The engagement of September 7th was the first operation by the Duxford Wing. On this occasion pilots of the three squadrons were credited with twenty enemy aircraft; No. 19 Squadron had claimed five destroyed and one damaged, and No. 310 had shot down five, probably destroyed five more, and damaged four. Considering that the *Hurricane* pilots were unable to attack in formation and were themselves attacked from above by *Bf 109's* and *Bf 110's*, their victory was remarkable. In contrast to the action of August 30th, considerable enemy fire was encountered from both bombers and fighters. Seven of No. 242's *Hurricanes* were hit, and Pilot Officer Crowley-Milling was forced to land away from base. Pilot Officer John Benzie in P2962 had been shot down and killed— the only fatality among the three squadrons involved. Once again the unit received a shower of congratulatory telegrams.

Bader and No. 242 were becoming the centrepieces of a controversy that raged through Fighter Command in the autumn of 1940. Essentially it was an argument between Air Vice Marshals Park (11 Group) and Leigh-Mallory (12 Group). It was 11 Group that bore the brunt of the German assaults that summer and fall, and 11 Group operated mainly with single squadrons scrambled to meet the incoming raids, often fighting against odds when large

20. Although some *Do 215's* operated during the Battle of Britain, it is far more likely that pilots claiming to attack this type were actually engaging *Do 17's*, which were far more numerous and virtually indistinguishable from the *Do 215*.

enemy formations were met. Leigh-Mallory believed in "big wings"—massed formations of four and five squadrons to overwhelm the German air fleets. He preached this concept to the harried Park. Bader, who held strong personal views on the desirability of such wings, became an instrument in the quarrel between the two senior officers.

The dispute between Park and Leigh-Mallory has been carried on by historians. Given the fact that the Battle of Britain was a defensive battle, pure and simple, the effectiveness of "big wings" was questioned then and later. It was Park's contention that such formations took too long to assemble and were too unwieldy in action, particularly in the situation faced by 11 Group, where major raids on forward airfields could develop at very short notice. This view has been supported without reservation by Wing Commander H.R. Allen and, to a lesser extent, by writers Derek Wood and Derek Dempster. An even stronger view is taken by Len Deighton, who condemned them as worse than useless but strangely over-rated. The kindest words for "big wings" (other than Brickhill's uncritical description) has been contributed by Francis Mason, who admits that such wings were not suitable for the conditions which Park had to handle during the early part of the Battle of Britain (the assault on Fighter Command stations). Once the *Luftwaffe* turned upon London, however, the wings were given the opportunity to assemble. Their impact upon German thinking was striking; at a crucial time, when the senior *Luftwaffe* staff believed the RAF to be down to its last *Spitfires* and *Hurricanes*, the appearance of large fighter formations shattered both illusions and confidence. Yet even Mason comments that the operational effectiveness of the "big wings" was much less than their proponents (Bader included) expected of them.[21]

On the night of September 7th the Germans delivered another punishing raid on London. Air action was relatively limited on the 8th, with another heavy attack on the capital that night. The morning of the 9th was also quiet, but that afternoon the *Luftwaffe* mounted several bombing raids on British targets.

21. Wing Commander H.R. Allen, *Who Won the Battle of Britain?* (London, 1974), pp. 114-120; Derek Wood and Derek Dempster, *The Narrow Margin* (London, 1961), pp. 195-197 and 272-273; Deighton, *op.cit.*, pp. 229-230, 260, 263-65; Mason, *op.cit.* pp. 231, 374, 389, 400.

No. 242 Squadron was scrambled at 5:00 p.m. in company with Nos. 19 (*Spitfires*) and 310. They had been airborne half an hour, patrolling between North Weald and Hornchurch while climbing for altitude, when specks began to appear at 22,000 feet. Enemy bombers were flying north across London; a box of some 60 German aircraft was followed by a similar box roughly a quarter of a mile behind and a bit higher. While No. 19's *Spitfires* attended to the latter formation, Bader led the two *Hurricane* units in a diving attack out of the sun and onto the leading bomber sections. *Bf 109's* in turn came down on the *Hurricanes* as they prepared to tackle the bombers. Several pilots turned to meet this threat, breaking up the enemy fighter formations.

McKnight was one of those who broke into the *Bf 109's*. A short-burst specialist, he sent one down in flames before two Messerschmitts came after him. He got between them, opened fire again, and saw one shed fragments before going down steeply. Another *'109* caught him with a burst, shooting off his left aileron. McKnight dived out of control and witnessed his second victim crash. Regaining control, he flew back to base.

Pilot Officer Latta also engaged a *Bf 109* from astern. At a range of 300 yards he fired for six or eight seconds. The Messerschmitt climbed steeply to the left and turned into a torch, the fire apparently coming from the cockpit area. Latta may have hit a fuel tank. The burning wreck spun away, but the Canadian had troubles of his own. His left aileron was hit and jammed; Latta escaped by diving and was not followed. Yet another *'109*, attacked by Flight Lieutenant Ball, exploded in mid-air.

Meanwhile, other pilots were harrying the bombers, identified as *Do 215's* but more probably the *Do 17's* of *Luftflotte 2*. Bader shot down one in flames and knocked holes in several others, weaving about among and below the Dorniers until his ammunition was exhausted. At one point he was caught amidst salvos of bombs as the Germans unloaded their deadly cargoes in their haste to get away. Powell-Sheddon, Richardson, and Lonsdale each flamed Dorniers as well. Lonsdale was caught in a crossfire by enemy gunners and his *Hurricane* was hit repeatedly, rendering his controls useless. With smoke, oil, and glycol pouring into his cockpit, Lonsdale baled out at 19,000 feet. He landed in a pine tree at Caterham, slightly injuring one leg. The tree stood on the grounds of a girls' school, and the students stood about giggling for half an hour before local police retrieved Lonsdale with a ladder.

Blue Section, probably in company with some of the Czechs of No. 310 Squadron, shot down two *Bf 110's*. One of these was a "flamer" credited to Pilot Officer Bush. The other two fell to Pilot Officer Tamblyn, who filed a dramatic Combat Report:

> Ordered off 1700 hours. E/A sighted 17.35. As we approached E/A from the east I saw 5 Me.110s detach themselves from the formation and turn in a right-hand circle towards rear of formation at 22,000 feet. I turned into an astern attack and noticed that a Hurricane was on the tail of a 110 which it set on fire. On the tail of the Hurricane was a 110 which fired a long burst at the Hurricane. I opened fire on the 110 whereupon it straightened up and after another burst both engines caught fire. I noticed one Hurricane with its port wing folding up and another machine which I took to be a Hurricane also with its port wing folding up.
>
> I went to the far side of the formation and climbed again. I saw a 110 making across me in a steep turn. I gave a short burst and went into dead astern where after a burst of about 7 seconds the port engine caught fire. The machine went into a fairly steep dive and I followed him down and watched him crash in front of a cricket clubhouse within one hundred yards of another crash near a burning house. There were many starlike spots on the ground which were perhaps incendiary bombs.

No. 242 Squadron had claimed a total of eleven enemy machines, to which could be added three shot down by No. 19 Squadron and four by No. 310. Yet these victories had not been without a price. Lonsdale, of course, had baled out safely after his *Hurricane* was hit. Pilot Officer Sclanders was not so fortunate. He was shot down and killed by *Bf 109's*. No. 310 lost three *Hurricanes* and one pilot in the battle.

On the 10th and 11th the squadron again operated from Coltishall, resuming its patrols over North Weald and London from Duxford on the 12th. There was nothing to report; weather restricted *Luftwaffe* activities several times, and the air battles of September 11th and 14th did not involve the "Canadian" squadron. Nevertheless, September 14th was an important day for No. 242; word arrived that Squadron Leader Bader had been awarded the Distinguished Service Order and Flight Lieutenant Ball had won the

Distinguished Flying Cross. These were the second and third gallantry awards won by members of the unit.[22]

Sunday, September 15th opened with mist but the weather promised to be fair. A few German reconnaissance sorties were reported. Shortly after 11:00 a.m. British radar plotters began detecting large numbers of hostile aircraft as *Luftwaffe* formations marshalled over France. Half an hour later one hundred *Do 17's* with their fighter escorts entered British airspace. At 11:25 a.m. No. 242 took off from Coltishall en route to Duxford. The famous "Duxford Wing" began assembling as well, bigger than ever, with five squadrons now—Nos. 19, 242, 302, 310, and 611. It was about 12:15 when this great mass of fighters encountered the German air armada over Gravesend. Everything went perfectly. The defenders had the advantage of height and sun; the three *Hurricane* squadrons (Nos. 242, 302, and 310) were flying line-abreast at 23,000 feet with the *Spitfires* of Nos. 19 and 611 stepped up at 26-27,000 feet. The enemy were at 17,000 feet, and the *Bf 109's* were glued so closely to the bombers that they had no opportunity to take the initiative. Moreover, the Duxford Wing was not alone; four other squadrons simultaneously attacked the German aircraft.

The battle was an incredible shambles, with no fewer than six enemy machines being shot down by No. 242 for the loss of one *Hurricane*. Other squadrons in the wing claimed twenty-three destroyed, eight probably destroyed, and several damaged. The air was thick with *Spitfires* and *Hurricanes* twisting about; Bader reported that he was seldom able to hold his sights on a target for long for fear of colliding with other fighters. Pilot Officer Tamblyn wrote that he twice had to wait his turn for a shot at a *Do 17*.

Bader, Cork, Stansfeld, and Turner each shot down a *Do 17*; another was destroyed jointly by Powell-Sheddon and Tamblyn. Neil Campbell damaged a *Do 17*. Norris Hart gave up trying to get at the bombers and bagged a *Bf 109* "flamer" instead. Flight Lieutenant Ball was slightly injured when he crash-landed his burning *Hurricane*. Two other aircraft of No. 242 had been holed, but the pilots were unhurt. The battle had been so well handled that Cork

22. See Appendix "A" for citations. Flying Officer G.P. Christie's DFC, announced on August 13th, had been for service with another unit prior to his reporting to No. 242 Squadron.

in his Combat Report paid tribute to Bader; "The success of the whole attack was definitely due to the good positioning and perfect timing of the C.O. of No. 242 Squadron."

The *Hurricanes* landed about 1:00 p.m.; their pilots kept busy reporting their combats and wolfing down lunches while the ground crews rushed to refuel and re-arm the aircraft. The Germans were busy too; another large raid began to assemble over northwestern France—150 bombers in three waves plus escorts. About 2:00 p.m. they commenced crossing the English coast on a ten-mile front. Fighter Command stations were the scenes of organized commotion as squadron after squadron became airborne.

No. 242 and the rest of the Duxford Wing were scrambled at 2:12 p.m. and began climbing through clouds while heading south. Again the *Hurricanes* flew in line-abreast formation while the *Spitfires* maintained station slightly above. The wing had reached 16,000 feet when anti-aircraft bursts pointed out the enemy bombers. This time the fighters were out of position; the Germans had a 4,000 foot height advantage. Bader started after the bombers, but then the enemy escorts began diving down. Detailing the *Spitfires* to carry on after the bombers, he ordered his *Hurricanes* to break up and engage the Messerschmitts. A whirling dogfight spread over Kent, between Kenley and Maidstone, as *Hurricanes*, *Spitfires*, Dorniers, Heinkels, and Messerschmitts mixed together, pilots and gunners opening fire at every opportunity.

At the beginning of the melee Pilot Officer Turner saw his bursts hit a *Bf 109*; the aircraft spun out of control. He believed that he had killed the pilot, but before he could determine the enemy's fate another section of Messerschmitts attacked him. A cannon shell exploded near his tail and threw him into a spin. As he pulled out below clouds Turner saw a *Do 17*. He attacked from the side, using full deflection. The starboard engine began to smoke and the bomber slipped into a gentle dive, hit the ground, and exploded between two houses on the north bank of the Thames. That was a "confirmed" victory; the '109 would be counted as a "probable".

A *Bf 109* made a firing pass at Pilot Officer Latta, missed, and overshot. Latta got on its tail and gave it a five-second burst from 50 yards. The '109 went down, burning and out of control, until it vanished into clouds at 5,000 feet. It would be assessed as "destroyed".

Pilot Officer Stansfeld was driven down. He sighted an *He 111* flying at 1,000 feet under attack by two *Hurricanes.* He joined in the chase, carrying out three attacks which stopped one of the Heinkel's engines. The bomber "pancaked" onto an aerodrome southeast of London where its five crewmen were taken prisoner.

In addition to these victories won by the Canadian members of the squadron, other pilots had shot down two *Do 17's* (one by Cork, one by Powell-Sheddon) and a *Bf 109* (Crowley-Milling). Although they had fought at a tactical disadvantage, No. 242 lost only one of the nine *Hurricanes* scrambled; Powell-Sheddon, having downed his bomber, was surprised by a *Bf 109* and shot down near Rye. He baled out with a dislocated shoulder.[23] The other squadrons of the Duxford Wing claimed twenty enemy machines destroyed for the loss of three *Spitfires*, two *Hurricanes*, and one pilot.

The events of September 15th were decisive. The *Luftwaffe* had lost 56 aircraft (the RAF claimed 185, but within a few days Fighter Command accepted a more realistic assessment; the public was not informed of the discrepancy until after the war). That punishment was bad enough, but more important was the obvious fact that Fighter Command was still alive and kicking. Bomber Command was also very much alive; the raids it launched against European ports filled with invasion barges were ample evidence. *Seelöwe*, scheduled to start on the 17th, was put off again, and the *Luftwaffe* cut back on daylight operations for two days.

For No. 242 Squadron the air battles of the 15th had a more local significance. With Powell-Sheddon in hospital, the unit needed a replacement "B" Flight Commander. Stan Turner was jumped from Pilot Officer to Flight Lieutenant and handed the job on the 16th.

The *Luftwaffe* tried to draw the *Spitfires* and *Hurricanes* into a general engagement on the morning of the 18th. There was little response from Fighter Command; the Germans had not produced enough bait to arouse interest. That afternoon the enemy raised the ante by throwing in a strong force of *Ju 88's* from KG 77, escorted by the usual swarms of *Bf 109's*.

No. 242 and the Duxford Wing were scrambled at 4:16 p.m.

---

23. Secondary sources differ on details of various actions, including this one. Powell-Sheddon's adventures are described here as set down by Wing Commander Hitchins and the Squadron ORB. Mason, *op.cit.*, p. 392, says that the Britisher was shot down by a *Do 17* he was attacking. Shores, *op.cit.*, credits him with another *Do 17* "shared with four other pilots" and one damaged.

They flew south toward London, climbing to 24,000 feet on the way. A thin layer of cloud at 20,000 feet obscured their view, so Bader descended to 19,000 feet. As he did so, anti-aircraft bursts drew his attention to two groups of bombers, each of twenty or thirty machines, 3,000 feet below and ahead of his fighters. There were no Messerschmitts about; the bombers apparently had lost their escorts en route to London.

Wheeling his squadrons about, Bader dived on the enemy as they flew up the Thames. The bombers stood out clearly against the clouds, and at the first shock of the assault their formations disintegrated. The raiders were scattered across the sky; a series of individual engagements followed as the *Ju 88's* were harried all the way back to the Channel.

"Willie" McKnight, flying as wingman to Bader, fired on a bomber that he identified as a *Do 17*; his aircraft recognition was almost certainly faulty. Its starboard engine caught fire and the crew baled out. In company with a *Spitfire* he then tackled a *Ju 88*. Both of its engines were knocked out, the crew took to their parachutes, and the bomber crashed in a field.

Neil Campbell was Bader's other wingman when they hit the enemy formation. In the ensuing free-for-all he overshot one target but soon had another in the form of a straggling *Ju 88*. He positioned himself astern and to port of the bomber, gave it a "squirt" at short range, and saw it go down with both engines burning. Campbell found himself on the starboard side of several bombers which were executing a turn toward him. He fired on the leading Junkers without effect, then tackled an *'88* previously mauled by a *Spitfire*. The pattern was familiar; both engines caught fire and the bomber went down in a precipitous descent. Campbell was still not finished. He overtook yet another *Ju 88* and damaged its starboard engine. His *Hurricane* was hit in the port wing, so he broke away; German defensive fire could be very hazardous. Next he teamed up with a *Spitfire* and together they sent a *Ju 88* down with both its engines on fire.

Tamblyn dived into the middle of the bombers, fired a burst, and then found himself in a dangerous situation where a crossfire could cut him to pieces. He broke out of the formation and did not see the results of his attack; it was McKnight who reported that Tamblyn had shot down a *Ju 88* in flames.

Norris Hart singled out a *Ju 88* and fired on it repeatedly,

P/O C.I.R. Arthur, a Canadian who was posted to No. 242 in December 1940, and his Hurricane which carried 'the Saint' as a personal emblem.

(C.I.R Arthur)

Pilots of No. 242, March 1941; P.S. Turner, K.M. Hicks (Australian), J.P. McKechnie (Australian), and C.I.R. Arthur.

(C.I.R. Arthur)

P/O N.D. Edmond, a Canadian who joined No. 242 in November 1940.
(C.I.R. Arthur)

A CBC interviewer speaks with F/O B.A. Rogers, F/L H.N. Tamblyn, and S/L W.P.F. Treacy, the CO who succeeded S/L Bader.
(Noel H. Barlow)

F/L M.J. Loudon and S/L W.W. Straight, flight commander and squadron commander of No. 242, May 1941.
(IWM)

P/O J.F. McKechnie and P/O F.E. Fayolle (French). (IWM)

F/L B.A. Rogers, F/O R.D. Grassick (the last of the original Canadians of No. 242), and P/O D.T. Kozak (Czech). (IWM)

S/L E.T. Smith, P/O D.K. Oak-Rhind (Australian), P/O J. Byrks (Czech). (IWM)

F/O C.I.R. Arthur and P/O K.M. Hicks. (IWM)

F/O Bruce Rogers and P/O F.E. Fayolle.   (Una Grassick via NMC)

F/L B. Duperier, whose book *La Vielle Equipe* gives much valuable information concerning No. 242 Squadron during the summer of 1941.   (Una Grassick via NMC)

Lt. Helge O. Mehre, one of three Norwegian pilots who joined No. 242 in June 1941.
                  (Major General H.O. Mehre)

Hurricane II LE.S, serial X2588, Spring 1941.   (C.I.R. Arthur)

30-minute readiness at the estate park near North Weald.
                                            (Maj. Gen. H.O. Mehre)

No. 242 officers and pilots, early **August 1941**. (*On ground, l to r*): F/O Baldwin, P/O H. Quilliam, S/L W.G. Wells, F/L Duperier, F/O Williamson, Sgt Kee, P/O J.P. McKechnie, Sgt Hull, Sgt. E.A. Redfern, P/O N.J. Luzemore, P/O K.M. Hicks. (*On aircraft*): F/O F.E. Fayolle, F/L Scitivaux, P/O R.F. Hamlyn, P/O J. de Pellepont, F/L E. Hagen. (Una Grassick via NMC)

Pilots and officers of No. 242 Squadron, early September 1941. The mascot is Pluto. (*Seated, l to r*): F/L Duperier, F/L Scitivaux, S/L Wells, P/O T.N. MacNamara, P/O J.P. McKechnie, "Bill". (*Standing*): Sgt H.C. Kee, P/O de la Bouchere, F/O Williamson, "Andy" (F/O Andrews?), F/L R.D. Grassick, Sgt Sands. (Una Grassick via PAC)

P/O Fayolle, P/O McKechnie, F/L Scitivaux.   (Una Grassick via NMC)

A relaxed group at dispersal with F/O Grassick in centre. With Bob Grassick's posting on 28 September 1941 the last link with the original No. 242 Squadron was broken.   (Una Grassick via PAC)

concentrating his bullets in the cockpit area. It caught fire and he followed it down, observing its crash near a railroad. Climbing to rejoin his comrades, Hart saw another *Ju 88* flying low on one engine. The eager Canadian pulled under the bomber and was in a near-vertical climb when he started shooting. The remaining engine began to burn, the Junkers rolled over, and the inevitable crash followed.

No. 242 had scored handsomely. Bader shot down two bombers, Ball claimed one, and so did Sergeant Brimble. Sub-Lieutenant Gardner was responsible for one bomber and also claimed a "probable"; he exhausted his ammunition in pursuit of stragglers. Pilot Officer Bush, the New Zealander, was credited with a "probable" *Ju 88*. He was unable to observe the fate of his victim because a *Spitfire* had gotten on his own tail, and though it did not fire, it also refused to be shaken off for several minutes.

The Commanding Officer had had an unusual combat. As he closed on one bomber (identified as a *Do 17* but probably a *Ju 88*) the rear gunner had baled out, apparently out of sheer fright, and had pulled his rip cord too soon. The parachute fouled the tailplane; the bomber fell out of control with the unfortunate gunner dangling behind. Two members of the crew got out safely. Bader fired a few bursts to put the gunner out of his misery but missed. The bomber plunged vertically into the clouds. "Once more", Bader wrote, "there seemed to be about three British fighters for every German, a most satisfactory state of affairs, if a little dangerous from the collision point of view."[24]

For the next six days (September 19th-24th) the squadron patrolled from Duxford with the 12 Group Wing, but had no combats. Bad weather then held it at Coltishall for two days.

---

24. The other squadrons claimed twenty "kills" and four "probables"; No. 19 claimed seven destroyed, No. 302 seven and three "probables", and No. 310 six plus one "probable". Double counting was bound to happen in this situation, but the battle of September 18th is particularly difficult to document. Mason, *op.cit.*, pp. 400-401, states that the entire wing destroyed only four bombers! Several German casualties of that day cannot be traced to specific RAF units, and may have been included in the Duxford Wing "bag". This writer's personal opinion is that German losses sustained at the hands of this wing amounted at least to roughly one-third of the total claimed, or about nine or ten enemy aircraft.

During this period the unit received three new fliers—Pilot Officers Roland Harold Dibnah and M.G. Homer, both formerly with No. 1 Squadron, together with Sergeant J.E. Saville, who came from No. 151 Squadron. They were experienced veterans; Dibnah already had a *Bf 110* to his credit and Saville had destroyed a *Do 17*. Dibnah came from Winnipeg; the others were British. All three reported to No. 242 on September 21st. Five days later Pilot Officer Cryderman also returned to the squadron after three weeks at No. 5 OTU.

There were occasions for celebrations as well. On September 24th notice came that Sub-Lieutenant Cork had been awarded a Distinguished Flying Cross; on the 27th it was announced that McKnight had been granted a Bar to his DFC, while Turner and Stansfeld had each won a DFC.[25]

Just before midday on September 27th the 12 Group Wing (now reduced to four squadrons—Nos. 19, 242, 310, and 616) left Duxford to patrol the London area. They were directed by radio to an enemy raid approaching across "Hell's Corner"—southeast of the Thames estuary. Turning southward, Bader presently sighted the enemy—twenty *Bf 109's* milling about in the Dover-Canterbury area at 18-20,000 feet. Once again the advantage lay with the British fighters, who had the sun at their backs and were at 23,000 feet with a cloud layer above to shield them from high-flying Messerschmitts. The wing achieved complete surprise; No. 242's pilots claimed four fighters destroyed, one "probable", and two damaged, while other squadrons in the wing claimed nine destroyed (seven of them by No. 19) and two "probables".

The most successful Canadian this day was Pilot Officer Latta, who shot down two yellow-nosed *Bf 109's*. He got on the tail of one Messerschmitt that was doing a steep turn. It levelled out and he delivered a three-second burst at 150 yards. Latta must have hit a petrol tank, for the German's cockpit was enveloped in flames; the *'109* dived vertically to earth, although the Canadian did not actually see it crash. He then sighted several Messerschmitts making for the French coast. As he still had the height advantage, Latta easily overtook them and fired at one from 250 yards. He kept on

---

25. See Appendix "A" for citations to these awards, and further discussion of Cork's decoration, which has been the object of some myth-making.

shooting until he had closed to about 150 yards; his target was hit in the fuel tank and went down burning. In his Combat Report, Latta wrote a few words that speak volumes about the intensity of aerial combat:

> My machine sustained damage to the tail and one wing through machine gun fire but I did not notice when this attack took place but imagine it was when attacking my first section. Enemy's idea of evasive tactics very poor steep climbs and turns only ones noted. Saw three other machines go down evidently out of control but could not confirm whether ours or theirs.

Hugh Tamblyn was driven down by a *Bf 109* to 10,000 feet. Having shaken off his pursuer, his attention was drawn by ack-ack bursts which fingered another '*109* heading back to France, evidently low on fuel. Tamblyn gave chase, snapping off bursts whenever his weaving target crossed his sights. Several times he scored strikes, and eventually the Messerschmitt began to stream petrol and glycol. Nevertheless, it was still airworthy when the Canadian broke off the action, his ammunition nearly gone, and so the claim was assessed as one "damaged".

Other claims against *Bf 109's* were submitted by Squadron Leader Bader (one destroyed, one probably destroyed), Pilot Officer Bush (one destroyed), and Flight Lieutenant Ball (one damaged). There was one other claim, this one for a *Ju 88*, submitted by Noel Stansfeld, who wrote a short, meaty Combat Report:

> I chased a ME.109 across Dover and then lost sight of this E/A. A JU.88 crossed my sights and then straightened out. I fired a burst at about 600 feet across Dover. The E/A then smoked and turned flying parallel to the coast on an easterly course. At about 50 feet my ammunition ran out (Damn it!). Due to bad visibility I was unable to confirm whether this E/A crashed. But I am convinced it had no chance of getting back across the Channel.

The Intelligence Officer was much more conservative; the claim was graded as "probably destroyed". There had been losses; Pilot Officer Homer had been shot down and killed near Dover. Two other *Hurricanes* were hit—those flown by Latta and Ball; the latter made a wheels-up landing with his engine on fire. No. 19 Squadron had lost two *Spitfires* with one pilot killed and one wounded;

No. 616 had lost one *Spitfire* with its pilot.

This action ended No. 242 Squadron's share in the heavy fighting during the Battle of Britain. It continued to patrol daily from Duxford and Coltishall but few enemy aircraft came within range. A tragic exception occurred on October 17th.

Red Section (Pilot Officers Campbell, Brown, and Rogers) was scrambled from Coltishall at 8:45 a.m. to patrol off Yarmouth. They were soon ordered to land, but that was cancelled and at 9:07 a.m. they were given a vector with instructions to fly at 7,000 feet. Eight minutes later they spotted a lone *Do 17* flying at 3-4,000 feet on a southerly heading.

The three *Hurricanes* swooped down. Rogers delivered a brief burst, then broke away to give his comrades a chance. Brown came in from dead astern and got off a short burst as well. An alert enemy gunner opened fire. The bullets hit Brown's throttle controls, jamming them open. He broke away, then, realizing he had lost sight of both Rogers and the Dornier, made his way back to Coltishall, landing at 9:50 a.m. Rogers meanwhile was hunting the bomber through clouds, catching glimpses of it but never able to close the range. He finally set course for base, landing at 10:20 a.m.

Pilot Officer Campbell never came back. He was shot down by the gunner who had damaged Brown's aircraft; the *Hurricane* crashed into the sea some 30 miles off Yarmouth. Later his body was recovered and buried on October 31st.

October saw some changes for No. 242 Squadron. The unit began moving to Duxford on the 19th, a shuffle which was slowed by weather and not completed until the 26th. Pilot Officer Stansfeld had gone to No. 229 Squadron on September 29th; Sergeants Lonsdale and Saville were posted out sometime after October 12th. New pilots on the squadron were Pilot Officer B.A. Rogers (September 28th or soon after), Pilot Officer J.G.P. Millard (October 17th, from No. 1 Squadron), Pilot Officer M.P. Warsham (October 17th), Pilot Officer C.B. Savory (October 18th, from No. 85 Squadron), Pilot Officer H.L.D. Kemp (October 18th, from No. 85 Squadron), and Pilot Officer J.J. Robinson (October 24th, from No. 85 Squadron). All of the new faces were British, and few stayed long. Warsham was reposted to No. 615 Squadron on November 3rd, and Savory and Robinson apparently did not stay long enough to fly any sorties with No. 242. In all the squadron had lost two Canadians (Stansfeld and Campbell) who were replaced by two British pilots (Rogers and Kemp). The "Canadian" squadron was clearly becoming less so.

No. 242 remained at Duxford until the end of November, when it returned to Coltishall. During this period it had only one engagement with the enemy, on November 5th. The squadron was patrolling over Gravesend-Sheerness at 27,000 feet in company with the *Spitfires* of No. 19 Squadron. A gaggle of *Bf 109's*, variously estimated to number ten to thirty, were seen above. Pilot Officer McKnight broke away and upward with his section to draw attention to the enemy.[26] He was still climbing, gamely attempting to reach the Messerschmitts' height, when the *'109's* put their noses down and attacked, firing quickly before zooming up to altitude again. McKnight was the only member of the squadron to fire. His Combat Report describes the action:

> Then one Me.109 dived down and was able to get behind, dived from 27,000 feet to 2,000 feet and gave one burst from approx. 150 yards. Pieces fell off and smoke came out, my machine was also covered in oil. Pilot of E/A then waggled wings and I flew up alongside and signalled him to land. He however opened his hood and jumped out. The machine crashed in Herne Bay and pilot landed by parachute in Herne Bay. Seen and confirmed by F/O Haines of 19 Squadron. Difficulty in aiming to fire was caused by front windscreen icing and fogging up. Cine camera gun was used. E/A coloured dark silver with a yellow nose.

Others were not so fortunate. Sub-Lieutenant Gardner, flying as wingman to Pilot Officer Latta, sustained bullet holes in his fuel tank and landed at Rochford. Pilot Officer Norris Hart, who was in Turner's section, was shot down and killed in P2806; in the confusion nobody saw him descending. As the *Hurricanes* headed back to Duxford, Squadron Leader Bader reformed with Cork and Latta to hunt for a Dornier reported by ground controllers. They flew up and down the Norfolk coast but saw nothing. All aircraft were

26. A general report of the action, apparently drawn up by Bader though unsigned, states that McKnight broke formation to investigate other aircraft which turned out to be *Spitfires*, a statement repeated by Hitchins in *The All Canadian Squadron*. McKnight's Combat Report states that he broke upward to attract Bader's attention to the enemy fighters; no radio problems are mentioned in either document.

down by 5:30 p.m.

"Willie" McKnight was undoubtedly No. 242's most deadly shot, but even he could put up the occasional "black". On November 19th, while flying the squadron *Magister*, he had to force-land at Luton. Having gotten the aircraft functioning again he took off, but without checking the weather forecast. Near Duxford the elements overtook him and he had to bale out. The incident led to a negative notation in his logbook by the station commander.[27]

The pilots were not the only ones to experience adventures. Squadron personnel drove a motley collection of vehicles that figured prominently in many stories. Noel Barlow and three other groundcrew bought a recalcitrant Triumph Eight from a WAAF who had been posted away. They patched it up, painted it red, white, and blue, and dubbed it "Funeral Freddie". With this they often drove into Norwich "for a few pints" and to other destinations.

Barlow had known Hugh Tamblyn from their Calgary days, and the latter sometimes borrowed "Funeral Freddie" to drive to the flight line. One day, without thinking to advise the owners, Tamblyn filled the tank with high-octane aviation gasoline. That night, as Barlow left the station for a date, the Service Police checked the tank, discovered the contents, and threatened to impound the car. The SP Sergeant on duty owed Barlow a favour, however, and consented to allow him out. Once off the station Barlow went to a local garage, exchanged the aviation gasoline for ordinary fuel, and thus got rid of the evidence. He thereby escaped 28 days detention— the standard punishment for raiding aircraft fuel stocks. "Funeral Freddie" died one day as its owner drove it from Coltishall to Birmingham on leave. Near King's Lynn it virtually collapsed, was pushed into a garage, and was abandoned as being beyond economical repair.[28]

Having moved from Duxford to Coltishall at the end of November, No. 242 moved again in December, this time to Martlesham

27. See Chapter 2, note 1.

28. Correspondence from Noel Barlow, September 1980. Barlow, a veteran of No. 242's adventures in France, was Mentioned in Despatches on January 1st, 1941—a rare distinction for a humble "erk".

Heath where it finished the year. The last few weeks of 1940 were spent primarily in convoy patrols, base patrols, and the training of new pilots.

Several new faces appeared in the squadron during November and December, and these were much more permanent than the people who had arrived in late October, most of whom had soon been transferred. The newcomers began with Pilot Officer Arthur William Smith, a native of Southport, Florida, though raised in Summerland, British Columbia. He arrived on November 4th, having previously served with No. 141 (*Defiant*) Squadron. Smith was followed by two English flyers—Pilot Officer O.E. Lang and Sergeant L.R. Thomas, who came from No. 6 Operational Training Unit on November 6th and 7th respectively. Another Canadian reported to the squadron on November 22nd—Pilot Officer Norman Douglas Edmond (Winnipeg-born, Calgary-raised), formerly of No. 615 Squadron. He had joined the RAF at the same time as Turner and Grassick.

November 28th brought two additional Canadian pilots, posted from No. 56 Operational Training Unit. Flying Officer Llewellyn Evan Price and Pilot Officer Donald Joseph McKenna were members of the RCAF, among the first representatives of the thousands of RCAF personnel who were to serve in RAF units during the war and the first in the squadron since the departure of Squadron Leader Gobeil. Price had been born in Quebec, served briefly with the Royal Rifles of Canada, and in January 1939 had enrolled in the Non-Permanent (or Auxiliary) RCAF. He had won his wings at Camp Borden on April 11th, 1940 and had gone overseas in September. McKenna, a native of Passaic, New Jersey, called Ottawa home; he had been trained at Camp Borden and received his wings on April 29th, 1940.

Another Canadian, this one a more familiar CAN/RAF type, reported on December 4th; he was Pilot Officer Joseph Adrien Deschamps of Rossland, British Columbia. He served only briefly with No. 242 as he was posted on December 30th to the Central Flying School, where he would die accidentally on January 17th, 1941. December 7th brought Pilot Officer Charles Ian Rose Arthur of Winnipeg, a member of the RAF since August 1938 and a former *Defiant* pilot with No. 141 Squadron. The last re-enforcements of the year were two exceptionally experienced Poles—Pilot Officers F. Surma and H. Szczesny, who arrived from No. 257 Squadron on

December 17th.[29] Neither of the Poles stayed very long with
No. 242 Squadron. Outbound postings occurred on December 30th,
when Pilot Officers Dibnah and Deschamps left the unit.[30]

29. Surma, who remained until March 1941, had shot down two aircraft and
probably destroyed one in the Battle of Britain. Szczesny had flown in the
Polish campaign and the Battle of Britain, and had shot down at least six German aircraft. He does not appear to have flown any operational sorties with
No. 242 before his posting to No. 317 Squadron at an unspecified date.

30. Dibnah rose to the rank of Squadron Leader and transferred to the RCAF
in 1945, having flown three operational tours.

1941:
Recessional

The beginning of 1941 brought a new period in the history of No. 242 (Canadian) Squadron. Hitherto, in the campaigns of 1940, it had been cast in a defensive role—protecting Allied troops in Belgium and at Dunkirk, covering the evacuation of the last British forces for the ports of western France, and guarding the skies of Britain against the massed assaults of the *Luftwaffe*. Now, in January 1941, it began to take part in the new offensive campaign launched by Fighter Command against German air units, aerodromes, and military installations in Occupied France and the Low Countries. No. 242 was no longer "all Canadian" in flying personnel, as it had been in the first half of 1940, but it was still fifty percent Canadian. As 1941 progressed, however, the Canadians became steadily fewer; by June the unit would be remarkably international in character.

Bomber Command, of course, had been on the offensive ever since the spring of 1940. Fighter Command had joined the effort on December 20th, when Flying Officer G.P. Christie (then with No. 66 Squadron, but late of No. 242) and another pilot shot up Le Touquet aerodrome. For No. 242 itself, offensive operations began on January 10th when Fighter Command undertook its first "Circus".

Six *Blenheims* from No. 114 Squadron were despatched to bomb the ammunition dump of Guines aerodrome near Calais. With them went 103 fighters from nine squadrons. No. 242 put up twelve *Hurricanes*; seven of the pilots were Canadians (Brown, Cryderman, Edmund, Latta, McKnight, Tamblyn, Turner). Together with No. 249 Squadron (also a *Hurricane* unit) they gave forward support by attacking St. Inglevert airfield. No. 242's pilots carried out their runs without seeing any targets of importance. No. 249's planes attacked some parked aircraft. That squadron lost one of their *Hurricanes* to a *Bf 109* which was shot down in turn; another '109 was destroyed by a *Spitfire* close to the bomber formation. The Canadian squadron had encountered no opposition other than some accurate anti-aircraft fire over the enemy coast.[1]

Two days later, with low cloud hanging over both England and the Continent, the squadron carried out three "Mosquito" raids—operations that would later be described as "Rhubarbs". Squadron Leader Bader and Flight Lieutenant Turner conducted the first of these. Taking off at 10:15 a.m. they flew over the English Channel at about 600 feet. Midway between Calais and Dunkirk they saw two enemy vessels—an "E" boat (motor torpedo boat) and a drifter (escort vessel, converted from or resembling a fishing boat). These were proceeding eastward. The *Hurricanes* turned about a mile ahead of the boats. In loose formation, Bader leading and Turner behind and to the right, they flew toward their floating targets. Bader, whose reports were invariably detailed and meticulous, described the attack:

> Both opened fire together at a height of 50 feet and speed 200 m.p.h. Saw bullets strike water ahead of "E" boat and then hitting "E" boat. Got one burst from front guns of "E" boat—no damage. "E" boat ceased fire. F/Lt. Turner having converged slightly on me, turned away to avoid slip stream as we passed over "E" boat. One burst from drifter before I opened fire and none as my bullets struck drifter. Passed over drifter and made for home with F/Lt. Turner in formation. Did not stop to observe damage to boats but

1. For detailed accounts of "Circus No. 1", see Michael J.F. Bowyer, *2 Group R.A.F.: A Complete History 1936-1945* (London, 1974), p. 164, and Peter Wykeham, *Fighter Command: A Study of Air Defence, 1914-1960* (London, 1960), pp. 183-84.

"E" boat must have had a lot as we could see bullets from 16 guns hitting the boat; drifter probably did not receive much damage—probably killed a few of the crew.

The pilots were exhilarated by this type of operation, offering as it did both action and the thrill of low-level flying. Bader and Turner had landed at 11:35 a.m.; at 12:15 p.m. four more *Hurricanes* took off, piloted by Flight Lieutenant Tamblyn, Flying Officers Rogers and McKnight, and Pilot Officer Brown. Twenty-five minutes later they split up over Gravelines; Tamblyn and Rogers turned east toward Dunkirk; McKnight and Brown headed down the coast.

The first pair flew over some fishing vessels apparently accompanied by an armed barge. Approaching the coast at 600 feet they saw tracer fire and turned westward, machine gunning a schooner and some small armed vessels. Rogers dived on one boat but seeing only one unarmed man on deck he did not shoot; the sailor stood and watched as the *Hurricane* roared past. En route home they passed over the fishing boats viewed earlier and fired at the barge. No hits were observed but four men were seen ducking down behind the railings. On landing Tamblyn discovered that his aircraft had been damaged slightly by a bird strike.

In the meantime Brown and McKnight had attacked an "E" boat and registered hits on its deck. Near Gravelines they crossed the coast. About a mile inland they saw a large concentration of troops, apparently entrenching and preparing machine gun emplacements. They strafed the enemy, causing them to scatter. The *Hurricanes* banked around for a second pass. Brown was trailing some 800 yards behind McKnight when he spotted a *Bf 109* astern, flying at 500 feet. Brown turned sharply to port, gave another gun site a "squirt", then looked around. Both the Messerschmitt and McKnight had vanished. Brown set course for base, landing at 1:15 p.m.

Flying Officer "Willie" McKnight, piloting P2961, did not return. He was dead, a victim either of flak or of the *Bf 109*. An original member of No. 242 Squadron, he had been its most outstanding Canadian pilot, shooting down at least sixteen (possibly eighteen) enemy aircraft and twice winning the Distinguished Flying Cross. His loss threw a pall of gloom over No. 242; it was front-page, banner-headline news in Calgary two days later.

The death of McKnight was not known when the next four *Hurricanes* took off at 1:25 p.m., flown by Cryderman, Arthur,

Latta, and Edmond. They picked up the French coast near Dunkirk and flew northward at 800 feet, just below the cloud base. As they did so they were subjected to anti-aircraft fire which crept up on them. As the four Canadians were weaving to avoid it, Cryderman became separated from his companions in the murk.

The three others tried repeatedly to reach Dunkirk again; at every approach they faced tracer fire and "flaming onions" (pom-pom flak) that flashed out of the mist. Near the Dyck lightship Arthur saw a *Bf 109*. The *Hurricanes* broke upward into cloud and lost touch with one another. Arthur and Edmond came home on their own. Flying Officer Latta, who had been flying V7203, another original member of the squadron, failed to return. Again, it is not known whether he was killed by flak or the *'109*. Cryderman, proceeding on his own, had shot up some shipping, evaded flak, and seen a lone yellow-nosed *Bf 109* appear and disappear in the mist. It may have been the same fighter reported by his comrades, or another.

The squadron had taken similar losses before. Nevertheless, January 12th, 1941, was one of the blackest days of its history. It had begun with high hopes for excitement; by late afternoon it had turned into shock with the double tragedy sustained in the loss of Latta and McKnight, prominent and popular members of the unit.

The remainder of the month passed relatively quietly. Snow-falls hampered flying on several occasions and the few operations carried out consisted of patrols over the base and coastal convoys.

At 2:00 p.m. on the afternoon of January 22nd, Squadron Leader Bader took off from Martlesham Heath, accompanied by Flying Officers Edmond and Cryderman. They were to cover a cruiser and submarine proceeding northward some fifteen miles off South-wold. The *Hurricanes* had been prowling their beat for about 50 minutes when Ground Control advised them to fly due east to inter-cept a "bandit". They followed instructions, but there was con-siderable haze. Several more vectors were given, and the course was changed to 330 degrees, then 340 degrees (roughly north-northwest), and finally to 30 degrees (north-northeast). At last they sighted a lone *Ju 88* some 500 or 1,000 feet above them. The fighters climbed to engage it.

The Commanding Office fired into the belly of the *'88*, which immediately unloaded its bombs, forcing Bader to swerve. Cryderman and Edmond began shooting up the target, crowding their chief out of the action. Cryderman, in his enthusiasm, very nearly collided with the tail of the Junkers when he delayed breaking away. Edmond exhausted his ammunition, after which Bader and Cryderman continued to harass the bomber until Cryderman's bullets were gone. Early in the engagement the *Ju 88* had emitted heavy orange and black smoke, but this had died away. Though the bomber flew rather erratically, it still seemed capable of getting home.

Bader flew alongside, then directed one last burst into the cockpit area. The *Ju 88* flew on. Abruptly, heavy orange smoke gushed from its port wing, followed by flames. The enemy machine went into a shallow dive that steepened noticeably before it went into the sea. In his report of the action, Bader wrote:

> The attacks made on the E/A were all from underneath or quarter attacks at very close range. Red 2 and Red 3, neither of whom had been in a conclusive combat previously, behaved like a couple of veterans, closing to very short range before firing, and firing very accurately.

The officers of No. 242 were honoured at the end of January; they were presented to King George VI and Queen Elizabeth as the royal couple visited Debden.

Fighter Command's offensive operations continued through February 1941. In addition to its routine of convoy and interception patrols, No. 242 was assigned to two sweeps across the Channel. On the 5th the squadron flew to North Weald for offensive action, only to have the operation "scrubbed" by weather. The other sweep, on February 15th, was uneventful.

The various patrols yielded more action. On February 3rd, Flying Officer Tamblyn chased a *Ju 88* over the Thames estuary but was unable to close to firing range. On the 8th, Flight Lieutenant Turner was scrambled with Flying Officers Cryderman and Crowley-Milling to investigate a "bogey" approaching a convoy off Felixstowe.

There was considerable cloud, but the trio located the aircraft, an all-black *Do 17*, some 40 miles east of Clacton. Despite machine gun fire from the bomber, Turner managed to clobber it in the starboard wing and fuselage, setting one engine smoking. He lost sight of the Dornier in the clouds, but twice on his radio he heard Cryderman call up that he was returning to base. A few minutes later

Cryderman reported that he was landing in the sea. His voice was normal; he did not sound wounded.

Turner gave up hunting the Dornier and began looking for Cryderman. He did not succeed. Subsequent searches also failed to locate the downed airman. His body was never recovered. There was no clue as to what had forced him to ditch, but one thing seemed probable—that Cryderman had believed himself to be only two miles off shore when he was actually more like thirty miles out to sea. His radio reports had simply confused the search.

Enemy aircraft were particularly active over England on February 15th. Flight Lieutenant Turner damaged a *Ju 88* over the North Sea that morning; Pilot Officer Crowley-Milling damaged another. Flight Lieutenant Tamblyn (who had been promoted on the 3rd) fired all his ammunition at a *Bf 110* but it eluded him after a long chase. In the afternoon Turner was vectored after a high-flying *Bf 109* but lost it in clouds. On February 19th Tamblyn and Flying Officer Smith, while patrolling off Orfordness, intercepted a *Ju 88*, but it also vanished into cloud.

Soon afterward the squadron lost another of its original members. On February 21st Flying Officer M.K. Brown, on a local flight in N2476, spun into the ground and crashed at Grange Farm. Only recently he had declined an opportunity to return to Canada as an instructor. It was reported that at the time of his death he still carried at least one bullet in his body from his wounds of May 1940.[2]

On February 25th, Flight Lieutenant Tamblyn engaged a *Ju 88* but lost it in clouds. During another patrol that day, in company with two other pilots, he spotted a *Do 17*, fired at it, and inflicted damage before it escaped into the clouds. The next day brought another incident. Flying Officer Arthur and Sergeant Redfern attacked a *Bf 110* some 30 or 40 miles out to sea from Orfordness. Once again, cloud cover enabled the enemy to flee before the *Hurricanes* could complete their task, but the Messerschmitt was sufficiently shot about that its starboard undercarriage dropped down and the wheel fell off.

At the end of February No. 242 Squadron began receiving

2. Toronto *Star*, February 24th, 1941; Toronto *Globe and Mail*, February 25th, 1941; James J. Halley, *Royal Air Force Aircraft—N1000 to N9999* (Tonbridge, 1977), p. 13.

Mark IIa *Hurricanes* with twelve .303 Browning machine guns as opposed to the eight guns in the Mark I versions. The first two months of 1941 had seen additional changes in personnel. New pilots were Sergeant A.J. Vaughan (arrived January 4th from No. 5 Radio Servicing Unit), Sergeants J.R. Pollard and E.A. Redfern (arrived January 29th from No. 232 Squadron), Pilot Officers J.M. Hicks, J.P. McKechnie, and D.K. Oak-Rhind (all from No. 56 Operational Training Unit, arrived February 18th), and Sergeants E.H.C. Kee and Jessop (posting dates uncertain; Jessop not further identified). Flight Lieutenant Ball was posted away on January 19th; his flight was taken over by Tamblyn. The two RCAF pilots, McKenna and Price, left for No. 110 (RCAF) Squadron on January 29th.[3] Through casualties and postings the unit had lost six Canadians. Of the newcomers, three were Australian (Hicks, McKechnie, Oak-Rhind); the remainder were British.

March was another quiet month; the daily round of patrols and one sweep passed without incident. During one sortie Hugh Tamblyn sighted a *Do 17* but could fire only once before it disappeared in cloud. Turner spotted a *Bf 110* during a morning patrol on the 14th, but it eluded him altogether. On the 27th he was subjected to British anti-aircraft fire while patrolling Felixstowe; fortunately his aircraft sustained no damage.

More important things that month happened back at base. On the 16th Squadron Leader Bader was promoted and posted to command the Tangmere wing. His departure was not a happy event for No. 242. In the minds of many the dynamic Englishman had become synonymous with the squadron, and he in turn had been generous in his public praise of them. In a broadcast on February 12th he had declared, "There has never been a snappier, more determined crowd of fighter pilots, and as an Englishman I am very proud to have the honour of leading them".[4] Behind the scenes he had worked hard for his men; several groundcrew succeeded in

3. McKenna later joined No. 403 Squadron; he was shot down over France on August 21st, 1941, and died of his injuries on September 8th. Price also went to No. 403 Squadron; he later served with Nos. 134 and 213 Squadrons. He was repatriated to Canada in July 1943. On January 21st, 1944, while flying a *Harvard* from No. 1 OTU, Bagotville, he was accidentally killed.

4. Toronto *Star*, February 13th, 1941.

remustering to aircrew through Bader's influence.

His place was taken by Squadron Leader W.P.F. Treacy, a Dubliner and veteran of No. 74 Squadron. Treacy harboured an intense, personal hatred of the Germans, a sentiment that had been bolstered when he had fallen into enemy hands and then escaped.

Pilot Officer Crowley-Milling was awarded the Distinguished Flying Cross in March, but it seemed that good news had to be cancelled out with bad. On the afternoon of March 28th, while patrolling over Clacton, Pilot Officer A.W. Smith crashed and was killed. He was buried at Ipswitch on the 31st.

The only other incident of note occurred on March 25th. Some *Bf 110's* bombed the airfield at Martlesham Heath. They did no damage to the aircraft, but hit a hangar that held some motor cars. Corporal Larry Stopforth fired at them with a machine gun; Corporal Albert Taylor was servicing a *Hurricane* when the raiders arrived. The latter was tempted to fire the guns of a stationary fighter at the Messerschmitts, but they made off before he could act.

April began auspiciously enough. On the afternoon of the 1st a section of *Hurricanes* led by Squadron Leader Treacy was scrambled to catch a "bogey" southwest of Lowestoft. It turned out to be a *Ju 88* flying at 7,000 feet. It immediately jettisoned its bombs as the fighters attacked. Cloud and the inherent toughness of the Junkers almost saved it, but Treacy and his wingman, Flying Officer Grassick, were tenacious; Grassick personally carried out four firing passes, receiving a bullet through his starboard wing and aileron for his troubles. The bomber went into cloud, emitting thick black smoke. Grassick followed it through the murk, and saw the *Ju 88* crash and burn.

While Treacy and Grassick harried their victim to its destruction, Flying Officer Edmond and Pilot Officer Crowley-Milling engaged another *Ju 88* that had apparently been shadowing the convoy they were guarding. Both pilots scored strikes, finally breaking away because their fuel was low and ammunition almost gone. They were credited with one damaged.

If things had begun well, April was soon to turn into a disastrous month. The *Ju 88* shot down by Treacy and Grassick was the only confirmed victory registered that month. On the other hand, six pilots would die in action or through accidents.

Convoy patrols occupied No. 242's attentions on April 3rd. At

6:00 a.m. Squadron Leader Treacy was scrambled with a flight and almost immediately encountered a *Do 17*. Treacy was flying a *Hurricane IIc*, armed with four 20-mm cannons, but his guns were troublesome. Two of them suffered stoppages, and in consequence the fighter's nose swung when a burst was fired. Treacy silenced a German gunner, knocked several holes in the bomber, and saw the engines streaming white vapour before he lost it in clouds. He was credited with one enemy aircraft damaged.

Two hours later Flight Lieutenant Tamblyn and Flying Officer Rogers took off to protect a convoy sailing east of Felixstowe. Anti-aircraft fire drew their attention to enemy aircraft, but in the clouds the two *Hurricanes* became separated. Rogers heard his leader reporting that he was about to make a head-on attack on a *Do 17*. The Englishman found a Dornier himself and fired six short bursts, but the range was too great for him to score strikes.

Tamblyn called up again, stating that he was on fire and was switching on "Pipsqueak", a homing device to enable ground stations to determine his position. Rogers looked briefly for the downed pilot, but then received instructions to return to base. A search by aircraft and launches soon found Tamblyn's body. He was unwounded, but had died of cold and exposure in the sea; his watch had stopped at 9:00 a.m. Just two days before his death he had attended an investiture at Buckingham Palace to receive his Distinguished Flying Cross.

Tamblyn's replacement as "A" Flight commander was Flight Lieutenant M.J. "Johnny" Loudon, a keen, cheerful Britisher whose good nature, it was said, left him only once. One day, ran the story, he refused to fly, declaring that "those bastards [the enemy] destroyed several thousand of my uncle's whiskey bottles in Glasgow last night"—the *Luftwaffe* having bombed that venerated city.[5]

Flying Officer Edmond was one of the keenest of the remaining Canadian pilots. On April 16th, when the squadron was detailed to conduct a sweep, he was delayed in taking off. Once airborne, Edmond was unable to overtake the others, so he conducted a lone sweep of his own along the French coast, strafing enemy troops before two *Bf 109's* chased him back across the Channel.

On April 20th the squadron had a busy schedule, with a sweep

5. Letter from Major General Helge Mehre, Royal Norwegian Air Force, to the author, July 6th, 1980.

over France and a patrol over the Channel. For the latter operation eleven *Hurricanes* took off at 1:30 p.m. They were at 21,000 feet, close to the North Foreland, when a string of unidentified aircraft was spotted. Squadron Leader Treacy began a steep turn away from these newcomers; in the process he collided with his wingman, Flying Officer Edmond. Both aircraft plunged toward the sea, followed by the remaining fighters. All was confusion; it was only after the survivors returned to base that they realized a third *Hurricane*, piloted by Flying Officer Lang, had also been involved in the collision. The bodies of Lang and Edmond were recovered; Squadron Leader Treacy had been utterly lost.[6]

The Air Officer Commanding, Fighter Command, Air Chief Marshal Sir Sholto Douglas, personally selected a new Commanding Officer for No. 242 Squadron. He decided that such a unit required dynamic leadership, in the Bader tradition, and chose Squadron Leader Whitney Willard Straight, MC, a former racing driver who had won his unusual (for a RAF pilot) decoration in the Norwegian campaign. The new CO arrived on the 23rd, and soon reported that he considered his cosmopolitan unit as "a bloody marvelous outfit".[7] Yet his debut was not auspicious. On the day that Straight reported to No. 242, Sergeant David was killed in a flying accident. Three days later, on April 26th, Sergeant Vaughan also died in a flying mishap.

Flight Lieutenant Stan Turner had been promoted to Squadron Leader and sent to command No. 145 Squadron on April 13th.[8] Not surprisingly, with the casualties suffered, many new pilots were posted to No. 242 in April and May, but only two were Canadians— Sergeant Marie Guy Alexandre Chase Casgrain (a former Montreal lawyer) and Sergeant George Alexander Prosser, a native of Brownsburg, Quebec who had been so proficient with handguns that he

6. Contemporary report, No. 11 Group Intelligence to Headquarters, Fighter Command, provided through the RAF Museum, Hendon.

7. Sholto Douglas, *Years of Command* (London, Collins, 1966), p. 136.

8. Turner ended the war with the rank of Group Captain, a DSO, and two DFC's. He was almost constantly on operations throughout the war, and stopped counting his victories somewhere around the fourteen mark. See H.A. Halliday, *The Tumbling Sky*, pp. 257-265 for a review of his career.

had narrowly escaped being allocated to air gunner training. Both were members of the RCAF. Others sent to the squadron included several British pilots, a Czech, and four Free French officers. Indeed, until the arrival of the two RCAF sergeants on May 5th, the only Canadians left in No. 242 were Flying Officers Grassick and Arthur. The latter was posted to No. 145 Squadron on May 23rd, further diluting "Canadian content".[9]

The "exiles" brought with them their own strange, and often tragic adventures of escape, and the hope that their homelands might be resurrected through their efforts. An instance was Francois Labouchère, whose father had been killed in action during the Battle of France. The younger man had been undergoing aircrew training when France capitulated. He had immediately asked his commandant for permission to fly to England. Refused, he fled to Morocco and from there had smuggled himself to England. "I have chosen to live proudly in misery", he said, "rather than accept shameful happiness." Labouchère would die in the pursuit of his own and his nation's honour.[10]

Throughout May the squadron continued its rounds of patrols over coastal convoys, Barrow Deep, Clacton, and the Thames estuary, operating first from Stapleford Tawney (a base to which it had moved on April 9th from Martlesham Heath) and then, after May 22nd, from North Weald, a few miles to the north. One of the "perks" of North Weald was a nearby estate owned by a Mrs. Dudley-Ward. It had a huge park where aircrew were invited to relax; indeed, they could sunbathe while at 30-minutes readiness. The estate also had a large pond, used both for swimming and for dinghy drills.[11]

The *Luftwaffe* had repeatedly bombed London during the winter, and on clear nights No. 242's *Hurricanes* had been scrambled in vain attempts to intercept. A particularly heavy blow was struck on the night of May 10/11. No. 242's pilots patrolled over London

9. Arthur was awarded the Distinguished Flying Cross in June 1944 for services with No. 72 Squadron. He rose to Wing Commander rank and remained with the RAF until 1954.

10. Bernard Dupérier, *La Vieille Equipe* (Paris, 1946), pp. 22-23.

11. See note 5.

from 10:00 p.m. until 4:00 a.m. This time they would enjoy outstanding success.

Pilot Officer Fayolle, one of the French pilots, had been scrambled with three other *Hurricanes* at 11:00 p.m. He was at 20,500 feet, flying in bright moonlight, when he sighted an *He 111* directly ahead. The bomber tried to escape by diving, but Fayolle could not be shaken off. He opened fire at 300 yards and closed the range to 50 yards, breaking away when oil from the bomber obscured his windscreen. The Heinkel caught fire, plummetted into the ground, and exploded.

Four more *Hurricanes* were scrambled at twenty minutes past midnight. Flying Officer Grassick flew at 20,000 feet, Flight Lieutenant Scitivaux at 20,500, Pilot Officer Kemp at 21,000, and Sergeant Kee at 21,500 feet. Visibility was 30 miles in a cloudless sky with a full moon.

Scitivaux was the first to see an enemy bomber—an *He 111* flying north. The Heinkel began turning to port as the French pilot made a port quarter attack. His first burst scored strikes, and oil from the bomber coated his windscreen. In subsequent firing passes he could barely see his target, although the bullets sparked as they struck the Heinkel. German gunners put several holes in the *Hurricane*. The *He 111* streamed smoke from one engine, its landing gear dropped, and it lost speed. Scitivaux lost contact while avoiding its defensive fire, but a few minutes later he observed an aircraft crash and burn. He was credited with the destruction of the Heinkel.

Grassick intercepted two more *He 111's* at 1:20 a.m., twenty-five minutes after Scitivaux had seen his bomber. This pair was at 19,000 feet, flying in the opposite direction to his fighter. He pursued one for several minutes until he was within range, then opened fire. He received some return fire from the Heinkel's gunners, but this soon ceased. After another long burst from astern the bomber's port engine began trailing white smoke. Grassick turned steeply to avoid overshooting the target, but nevertheless lost his quarry in the darkness. He claimed a "probable".

No. 242 continued to fly offensive sorties; on May 14th Squadron Leader Whitney Straight led three *Hurricanes* in a very effective "beat-up" of Ostend/Middelkirke aerodrome. Approaching their objective in the predawn light, the pilots split into pairs, each team having a cannon-armed and a machine gun-armed *Hurricane*. Straight and Oak-Rhind made the first pass at 100 feet, followed by Loudon and McKechnie. They saw no enemy aircraft on the airfield, but inflicted casualties to personnel, shot up some gun positions, and touched off an explosion in a hangar. En route home they observed three *Bf 109's* looking for them, but these were avoided.

If May had its successes, there were losses as well. A week after the attack on the Ostend/Middelkirke field, No. 242 undertook a sweep with No. 56 Squadron in the St. Omer-Gravelines area. *Bf 109's* attacked, shooting Pilot Officer Oak-Rhind down into the Channel.

No. 242's Canadian contingent remained at three men throughout June—Grassick, Casgrain, and Prosser. New pilots continued to be about half British, half other nationalities. On June 2nd three Norwegian Air Force pilots arrived—Captain Odd Bull and Lieutenants Egil Hagen and Helge Mehre. All had trained in Canada before proceeding to Britain. Mehre later recalled his surprise at the number of nationalities in the squadron, particularly when he discovered that the unit was designated as "Canadian".

> From our broad experience of co-operation with the RCAF in the Norwegian Training Camp "Little Norway" in Toronto we soon felt "at home" with the Canadians and the Canadian "atmosphere", and of course with all the other pilots and men who adhered to the Canadian "tone". Another early observation which made a lasting impression was the excellent formation flying of the squadron.[12]

The tempo of fighter operations increased in June. No. 242 Squadron, while continuing its routine of convoy, Barrow Deep, and night patrols, participated in nine "Circuses" and sweeps over enemy-occupied territory; Grassick took part in eight. These led to more engagements than the pilots had had for many months past; five enemy aircraft were destroyed, a sixth shot down and shared with another squadron, five probably destroyed, and ten damaged. Three pilots went missing; another was killed in a crash.

The most unusual action was a lone intruder sortie flown by Squadron Leader Straight. On the night of June 12th he took off from Manston, arriving at Merville airfield close to midnight. The field was brilliantly lit. He detected and stalked a *Bf 110*, shooting it down with one burst of cannon fire. Straight remained in the area

12. See note 5.

for a further thirty minutes, chasing and losing another '110. Despite his obvious presence, the airfield lights remained on until he strafed the control hut.

Most of No. 242's action that month, though, occurred during a "Circus" to Bethune in the early evening of June 17th. No. 242, together with Nos. 56 and 306 Squadrons, was detailed as close escort to twenty-four *Blenheims* that were to bomb the Chocques chemical works. Rendezvous was made at 7:00 p.m. over Southwold. Twenty minutes later they crossed the French coast and headed inland.

Unfortunately, the top cover had been ordered to fly at a very high altitude and was not in a position to help the escort wing. About fifteen miles from the target three *Bf 109's* appeared and made several zooming attacks on the *Hurricanes*, shooting down Pilot Officer Byrks (Czech). Over Bethune itself fifty to seventy *Bf 109's* joined in the fray. The *Luftwaffe* must have sent up practically every fighter it had in northwestern Europe for this battle, as the German attack on Russia was only five days away. A series of dogfights ensued. Flying Officer Grassick's Combat Report describes the intense, confused action:

> One passed immediately under me heading for the tail of the last section of bombers. I opened up full throttle but he pulled away from me. By this time I was opposite the tail end of the bombers. Just then another Me.109 attacked the last section of the bombers and turned to the starboard side. I moved over and had a good 2 seconds burst at him starting from about 150 yards until he pulled away from me. I saw white smoke coming from him and he turned slowly away more to the starboard and back toward the way from which he had come. Then saw bullets hitting my wings so took certain evasive action and shook him from my tail. I then moved back to my former position near the tail end of the bombers about 500 feet above. While watching another Me.109 (old type—square wing tips) came up to attack bombers, so I turned on to him and at about 200 yards opened fire and slowly closed in on him and saw white and black smoke pouring out and he dived steeply towards the ground, completely out of control. I then found I had another on my tail and after shaking him off saw another coming up on the bombers so turned and took a quick shot

but he turned away and I saw no definite result. I resumed my original position and saw the bomber formation safely over the English coast . . . When returning I saw a pilot bale out of a Hurricane over France and 25 miles S.E. of Boulogne.

Grassick was credited with one *Bf 109* destroyed and one probably destroyed. Straight had claimed a "probable" and one damaged, while "probables" had also been credited to Pilot Officer Kemp and Sergeant Redfern. Other pilots damaged a total of six Messerschmitts. The battle had been savage; nine escorting fighters had been shot down. No. 242 alone lost three pilots—Byrks, Squadron Leader E.T. Smith (supernumerary, attached to the unit since April 28th), and Flight Lieutenant B.A. Rogers (who had been with the unit since October 1940). In spite of the efforts of the *Hurricanes*, the bombers had been hard pressed; one *Blenheim* was attacked six times by *'109's*, though it survived to belly-land at Horsham.[13]

Byrks was the second Czech to die in three days; in the morning darkness of June 14th Pilot Officer Kozak had been blinded by searchlights just as he landed and had been killed in the crash that followed. Among some pilots the theory eventually evolved that "They go by nationalities", citing the Czechs as the first victims of such a pattern.[14]

During another "Circus" to St. Omer on June 21st, escorting six *Blenheims* of No. 21 Squadron, *Bf 109's* again intercepted. Lieutenant Mehre, one of the new Norwegian pilots, damaged one Messerschmitt and witnessed the loss of a *Blenheim*. Whitney Straight crippled a *'109* that was finished off by a *Spitfire*; he was awarded half the victory.

On the following day No. 242 despatched twelve *Hurricanes* as part of the escort for another *Blenheim* formation. On the homeward flight they escorted a damaged *Spitfire*; when its pilot baled out near the English coast Pilot Officer Hicks followed him down, not leaving until a rescue launch arrived. About the same time Flight Lieutenant J.E.F. Demozay attacked two *Bf 109's* that in turn were stalking some *Hurricanes*. He shot one down into the sea, fought

---

13. Additional details from Bowyer, *op.cit.*, pp. 171, 175, 498.

14. Dupérier, *op.cit.*, pp. 37. The writer of that book overstated his case by mentioning the loss, first of the Czechs, then of Poles, followed by a double Canadian loss. In fact, there were no Polish casualties among No. 242 personnel that summer of 1941.

the second for five minutes, and lost it when he blacked out in a steep pull-up.

June 23rd brought another sharp, successful action for the squadron. During the battle, fought near Mardyck aerodrome, Demozay repeated his feat of the previous day, destroying a *Bf 109*; another was shot down by de la Bouchère. Flight Lieutenant Grassick, leading the squadron escort to six *Blenheims*, fired bursts at two enemy fighters which had dived out of the evening sun. One went down smoking (probably destroyed) while the other was hit and claimed as damaged. Sergeant Redfern damaged yet another *Bf 109*.

The month concluded with three more escort missions. There was no contact with the enemy, other than the customary intense and accurate flak so frequently provided by the Germans. Grassick now held a senior position with No. 242; he had been promoted and made a Flight Commander in mid-June, succeeding Rogers, who had been lost in action on the 17th.

"Circuses" were again the chief operational activity of the squadron during the first half of July; its pilots participated in ten such missions in the course of eighteen days, visiting Lille (twice), Bethune, Abbeville, Hazebrouck (twice), and St. Omer. *Stirling* bombers of Nos. 7 and 15 Squadrons formed the striking force on most of these occasions. One wonders at times why the RAF bothered with these sweeps, and why the *Luftwaffe* honoured them with any opposition at all. On July 5th, for example, the RAF sent three *Stirlings* to bomb steel works at Lille, and surrounded this meagre force with no fewer than sixteen fighter squadrons. For the same operation, as a diversion, a single *Stirling* went to bomb Abbeville marshalling yards with three fighter squadrons—Nos. 71, 242, and 222. While the main group encountered enemy fighters, the diversionary force was left alone. The *Stirling* casually dropped eighteen 500-pound bombs on the target, probably inflicting no more damage than a good railway crew could repair within forty-eight hours.

A similar operation was carried out on July 7th, when one *Stirling* was sent to bomb Hazebrouck marshalling yards. Nos. 71, 222, and 242 Squadrons accompanied the "heavy" throughout its sortie, and saw no enemy aircraft. Eight other fighter squadrons supported the operation; Nos. 64 and 603 Squadrons tangled with some *Bf 109's*.

There were occasions when No. 242 had its turn at the enemy. On July 4th, during an attack by twelve *Blenheims* on Bethune, several *Bf 109's* tried to engage the bombers and heavy fighting erupted, with several individual dogfights raging. Three Messerschmitts were shot down by Hamlyn, Loudon, and Mehre, two were probably destroyed (Orton, Hicks), and three were damaged (McKechnie, Hicks, and Hagen). The *'109* destroyed by Mehre was the first "kill" credited to a Norwegian in the RAF, and he subsequently described the event on the BBC home service and Norwegian broadcasts.

Another sweep on July 6th produced good results. No. 242 was escorting six *Stirlings* raiding the Lille steelworks. Shortly after the bombs had been dropped, *Bf 109's*, operating singly and in pairs, began attacking. In a head-on pass Dupérier fired a burst that crumpled the tailplane of his opponent; he claimed a "probable" that was later upgraded to "destroyed". Mehre damaged a *'109*. Two other pilots fired without success; among these was Sergeant Prosser, one of the Canadians.

On the 8th No. 242 was out once more, escorting three *Stirlings* to Lille. The raid itself was a failure; intense flak damaged all three bombers and forced them to take evasive action that spoiled their aim. Normal fighter opposition was met; Sergeant Redfern damaged a *Bf 109*.

On July 19th the squadron abruptly moved from North Weald to Manston, the airfield built at the edge of the coastal cliffs and reputed to be within range of heavy German guns in the Pas de Calais. A new role had been assigned to them—that of protecting and supporting *Blenheim* bombers during daylight attacks on coastal shipping.

Operation *Channelstop* was in progress. This was an attempt to halt all ship movements from Holland to the Seine River through air power. Ultimately it was recognized that the effort was unsuccessful; claims of vessels sunk or damaged were too optimistic. The campaign did disrupt enemy sea transportation to some degree, mainly by compelling ships to move by night and tie up by day.

It had been quickly recognized that the principal hazards for *Channelstop's* low-flying bombers were the flakships the enemy mixed with their convoys. The term "flakship" conjures up images of powerful warships. In fact such vessels were frequently small craft—trawlers and motorized barges—which nevertheless bristled with light- and medium-calibre anti-aircraft weapons. In part they were dangerous because they were relatively inconspicuous. The task of No. 242's *Hurricanes* would be to rake the decks of the flak ships, keeping the enemy gunners' heads down while the *Blenheims* went about their work.

The squadron conducted the first such operation on the evening of the 19th, silencing a flak ship that had been escorting a 6,000 ton tanker off Ostend. Two similar missions were completed on the 20th when more enemy ships were hit. During the second strike No. 242 accompanied six *Blenheims* to Berck-sur-Mer. A tanker was set on fire, but two bombers were lost. Two *Hurricanes*, piloted by Grassick and Mehre, were damaged by flak, while Dupérier narrowly escaped being shot down by *Bf 109's* that attacked him by surprise (he had taken them to be *Spitfires*) and riddled his fighter without crippling it.[15]

Again on the morning of the 21st, No. 242 Squadron escorted *Blenheims* on a strike at Boulogne and left a ship burning. Later in the day the pilots attacked and hit an "R" boat (fast minesweeper). Another strike, against a tanker off Ostend on July 23rd, had tragic results. The enemy, profiting from experience, placed four flak ships around the main vessel. They directed little fire at the *Hurricanes*, concentrating instead on the bombers. Four of the six *Blenheims* engaged were lost. Their bombs were reported to have straddled the target and one may have scored a direct hit. Even so, the tanker escaped.

On July 27th the squadron despatched twelve *Hurricanes* (four armed with cannon, the others with machine guns). A German destroyer had been reported northeast of Calais and British motor torpedo boats were being sent to attack it. The pilots found the destroyer, escorted by five E-boats and at least eight *Bf 109's*, but at no time did they see the British naval force. *Hurricanes* and Messerschmitts paired off into dogfighting groups. Flight Lieutenant Hamlyn found two '109's in front of him and shot one into the sea. Squadron Leader Straight attacked several Messerschmitts; he claimed two "probables" after they streamed heavy black smoke. Another "probable" was credited to Pilot Officer McKechnie,

15. Dupérier, *op.cit.*, p. 31-32. According to Hitchins and the logbook of Mehre, all three damaged *Hurricanes* were hit by flak.

whose target lost oil and appeared to be out of control before vanishing in haze. Flight Lieutenant Grassick fired at a Messerschmitt without effect. One *Hurricane* was lost, and with it went Sergeant Prosser, one of the Canadians on strength. He was seen to take evasive action after a '109 attacked him; his fighter spun into the sea.

On the last day of the month another shipping strike was attempted, but the bombers were unable to locate their target and turned back. The *Hurricanes* continued their patrol to Fecamp where they attacked a destroyer and other escort vessels in the face of an intense barrage of flak. Squadron Leader Straight's aircraft was hit by concentrated 20-mm fire. He radioed, "Good luck boys. See you soon again. I'll be back," after which he crash-landed in France. He was as good as his word. After many adventures, including imprisonment in Vichy, France and his subsequent escape, he would make his way back to England, thanks to his command of French, sheer effrontery, and iron determination.[16]

His successor, Squadron Leader W.G. Wells, arrived on August 1st. That day saw another Canadian lost. Returning in bad weather from a "Roadstead" (shipping strike). Sergeant Casgrain was mistakenly attacked by a *Spitfire*. The pilot of the latter fired a brief burst, realized his error, and broke away. His guns had operated less than two seconds, but in that interval Casgrain was killed. By a strange and tragic twist of fate the *Spitfire* pilot was also a Canadian, a member of the RAF who would survive the war with a very distinguished record. The only Canadian now left in No. 242 was Flight Lieutenant Grassick, who had been with the unit since its formation.

Anti-shipping strikes continued to dominate No. 242's activities. Sometimes they escorted bombers; on other occasions they conducted strikes on their own. August 3rd was a particularly busy day involving three distinct operations. Just before noon twelve *Hurricanes* took off from Manston, strafed several vessels near Gravelines, and were back at base 35 minutes later. In the late afternoon a pair of Australians, Hicks and McKechnie, was sent to attack an E-boat reported near the English coast. They did not locate it, but found

16. Dupérier, *op.cit.*, p. 33. Sholto Douglas, *op.cit.*, p. 138, describes the loss of Straight as a personal shock. He reports the parting message as, "I have been hit, am going to force-land in France", after which he ordered the squadron home.

two *Bf 109's* instead. With height and surprise in his favour, Hicks closed on one Messerschmitt and followed it to the French coast, snapping off short bursts. The German took no evasive action and finally crashed. At 5:55 p.m. nine more *Hurricanes* were scrambled to hunt E-boats in the Cap Gris Nez area. One such vessel was found; Flight Lieutenant Scitivaux strafed it twice with his 20-mm cannons and set it burning. A tug or trawler was also fired upon.

Not all operations could be so successful. On August 10th No. 242 supported three *Blenheims* on a strike. Two of the bombers were shot down and the third came home with most of its crew wounded. Pilot Officer de Pellepont was also lost, probably hit by a *Bf 109*. His death led to some anxiety among the Free French pilots, by this time ruled by the superstition of casualties by nationalities.

A particularly intense action took place in the early evening of August 17th. Eighteen *Hurricanes* (twelve from No. 242 Squadron, six from No. 3) left Manston in company with three *Blenheims* from No. 18 Squadron. After picking up two squadrons of *Spitfires* for cover, the formation set course for Le Touquet, where a 5,000 ton motor vessel had been reported. The *Blenheims* and *Hurricanes* flew at less than 100 feet until they spotted the target with its complement of flak ships. As the fighters engaged the escort vessels, several *Bf 109's* appeared. Pilot Officer Quilliam shot down two with only six seconds of cannon fire; pilots in No. 3 Squadron claimed one probably destroyed and two damaged. On the other hand, two *Hurricanes*, piloted by Hicks and Redfern, were shot down; one of them was last seen on fire, trying to make the French coast. Faced with intense opposition, the *Blenheims* turned away and did not bomb the target.

Hicks had been one of the Australian pilots. Two days later the theory of serial casualties received further substantiation. Twenty-two *Hurricanes* from Nos. 1, 3, and 242 Squadrons attacked shipping in Ostend harbour. It was a confused affair in which many barges and drifters were fired at, but no concerted attacks were made; the pilots kept finding other *Hurricanes* coming from all directions. Ship and shore flak was liberal. Early in the attack Pilot Officer McKechnie was hit; he baled out, came down in the sea, and was later picked up and taken prisoner. McKechnie was the second Australian lost in three days.

Operation *Channelstop* was having some effect; enemy sea movements by day were diminishing. Yet to be effective, the RAF had to maintain the pressure and take whatever casualties resulted. In consequence, No. 242 suffered yet another loss on August 26th, when Pilot Officer Quilliam was shot down while attacking an E-boat. Pilot Officer Lezemore was accidentally killed on the 29th.

Rumours abounded that No. 242 was about to be re-equipped with *Typhoons*. The pilots looked forward to such an event; they had not heard of the teething troubles being encountered with that type. Meanwhile, the war took some odd twists. On August 25th a party of Canadian sappers visited Manston. Bernard Dupérier recorded that they brought with them *"des machines d'apocalypse"*. They mined the airfield with explosives wired to an electric detonator. One year after the Battle of Britain the authorities had finally readied Manston for destruction to prevent its use by the enemy![17]

Postings brought several changes that month. The three Norwegian pilots—Bull, Hagen, and Mehre—were transferred on August 8th to No. 331 (Norwegian) Squadron which had just been formed. There was a considerable flow of replacements, and on August 23rd three Canadians arrived. Pilot Officer Clifford Elmer Sluggett, a native of Victoria, was a member of the RAF; he had been commissioned from the ranks on June 1st. Sergeants Herbert Hale (Toronto) and Ray Vernon Harvey (Deseronto, Ontario) were both members of the RCAF and graduates of the British Commonwealth Air Training Plan.

No. 242's two final shipping strikes were flown on September 2nd; each lasted an hour. *Blenheims* hit a tanker while the *Hurricanes* attacked flak ships, setting one on fire, and drove off several *Bf 109's*. All four Canadians on strength took part in both these operations. The last operational casualty occurred on the 10th, when Sergeant Reilly failed to return from an early morning weather patrol.

No. 242's active days in Europe were drawing to a close. On September 13th the squadron moved to Valley, Angelsey; No. 615 Squadron replaced them at Manston. Under the circumstances there was a good deal of posting back and forth between the two units. Five pilots (including the three Free French pilots with No. 242)

17. Dupérier, *op.cit.*, p. 42.

transferred to No. 615 to stay in the battle, while twelve of No. 615's pilots were switched to No. 242, some for short-term postings and others for longer periods. Thus, for a brief period, two additional RCAF pilots joined the squadron. They were Sergeants Case and Spencer (not further identified), who came from No. 615 on September 22nd and were reposted to other duties on the 27th.

Many changes had occurred among the groundcrew as well. As of May 1941 some forty-six Canadian tradesmen were still with the squadron. From that time onward, however, Canadian "erks" rapidly departed on other postings, some to more advanced technical work, others to aircrew training. Squadron Leader Bader had pushed hard for several men seeking to remuster to flying duties, including three who had personally serviced his *Hurricane*—Albert Taylor, Dale Stephens, and Edward Cameron.[18] Their places were taken by British personnel with only short courses in line maintenance behind them. Few Canadians were sent to No. 242 as airman replacements; most CAN/RAF "other ranks" had joined at a time when training was very thorough, and they were already moving to other trades or levels. RCAF airmen were not available; they were required for the growing number of Canadian squadrons in Britain.

In its new base the squadron was concerned only with convoy patrols. Flight Lieutenant Grassick travelled to London where he was invested with the Distinguished Flying Cross on September 23rd. His last appearance in No. 242's records was on September 28th when he flew a convoy patrol. Shortly thereafter he was posted to No. 73 Operational Training Unit, Aden. He had been with No. 242 since November 1939, and his departure severed the last link between the existing squadron and its old "Canadian" form of 1939-40. On October 5th the unit was ordered to stand down and was then declared non-operational. Preparations began for its eventual move overseas.

18. The subsequent careers of these three may be taken as typical of those remustering to aircrew. Taylor became a pilot and attained the rank of Flight Lieutenant. In 1944, while flying agents in and out of enemy territory, he was ambushed and wounded by German troops but managed to take off and escape. Stephens took pilot training in the United States and flew two operational tours with Nos. 403 and 122 Squadrons; he took part in 157 sorties and shot down two enemy aircraft. Cameron won his wings in 1942 and became a bomber pilot with No. 78 Squadron. All three survived the war; Stephens and Cameron served in the postwar RCAF.

During the period of November 1939 to October 1941 one hundred and fifty pilots had served in No. 242 Squadron, of whom forty-two were Canadians (six of them RCAF). Of that number, twenty-four Canadians had been killed or taken prisoner in the course of flying operations. They had won one Bar to the Distinguished Flying Cross and six Distinguished Flying Crosses. Of the 105½ enemy aircraft officially credited as destroyed (87 in 1940, 18 in 1941), the Canadian pilots had accounted for 47 (all but two in 1940) and shared in the destruction of eight more. In addition, several "unofficial" victories had been registered by Canadian pilots during the Battle of France—unofficial in that they had not been recorded in squadron diaries or Combat Reports, although they had been mentioned in after-battle accounts and letters. It was a fine fighting record; the squadron as a whole and its Canadian members in particular had lived by the motto of the unit: *Toujors Pret—* always ready.

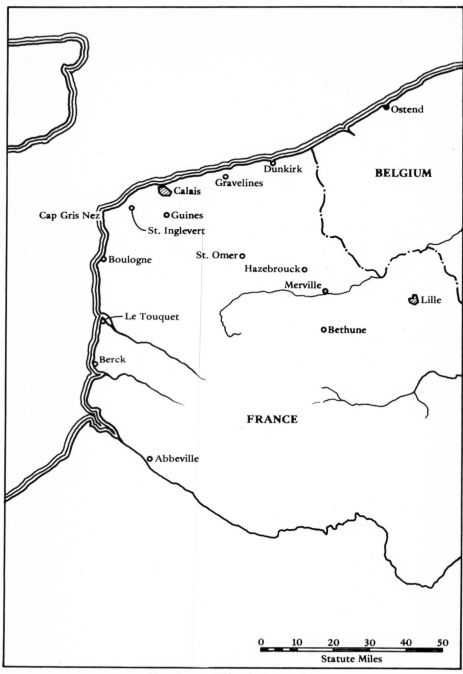

**Map 5 - Offensive operations
1941**

Epilogue

The subsequent fate of No. 242 Squadron is worthy of description. On October 3rd, 1941 the unit was declared non-operational and prepared to move to the Far East. The men embarked in December, sailing for Gibraltar. Several pilots and aircraft were put aboard a carrier, which conveyed them to the Central Mediterranean. They flew to Malta, but instead of continuing onward they were detained to aid in the defence of that island. They included Pilot Officer Slugget, who was wounded on January 25th, 1942, and Sergeant Harvey, who was killed in action on March 1st, 1942. Both were still nominally on the strength of No. 242, although that unit was half a world away at the time.

The balance of No. 242 continued round the Cape of Good Hope and arrived in Sumatra early in January 1942. Fighting alongside Nos. 232, 258, and 605 Squadrons, they were caught up in a hopeless campaign. Japanese *A6M Zero* fighters outclassed the *Hurricanes*, and on February 14th their airfield was attacked by enemy parachutists. The *Hurricanes* escaped to Java while many of the ground personnel evaded capture. As the battle continued, units merged to maintain a minimum number of aircraft operating. By March 6th No. 242 was down to five *Hurricanes*. These remained in

Java, continuing to fight until the island was overrun. Two Canadian airmen—Corporal W. Yeardye and Aircraftman V.E. Syrett—were captured during this campaign. No. 242 ceased to exist.

On April 10th, 1942, a new No. 242 was formed at Turnhouse, Scotland, equipped with *Spitfire V's*. The squadron was declared operational on June 1st. Two days later the pilots registered their first claim—a *Ju 88* probably destroyed east of Drem by Flight Sergeant John Maxwell Portz, a member of the RCAF who hailed from Weyburn, Saskatchewan. It was both fitting and ironic that a Canadian should draw first blood for the new squadron, which was in no way intended to be as "Canadian" as the original unit had been.

The next few months were largely uneventful, apart from ground support duties during the Dieppe raid of August 19th. In October, however, they embarked for overseas duty once more, this time to participate in *Torch*, the Allied landings in North-West Africa. They arrived at Maison Blanche, Algeria, on November 9th. Throughout the following campaign they saw considerable action in which Portz, who had been commissioned, probably destroyed a *Ju 88*, shared in the confirmed destruction of two more, and damaged three *Bf 109's*.[1] On March 9th, 1943, Flight Lieutenant C.I.R. Arthur was posted to the unit as a Flight Commander; two years before he had been one of the Canadians serving with No. 242 in England.

With the end of the North African campaign, No. 242 Squadron moved to Malta. The *Spitfires* escorted bombers that were "softening up" Sicily, and when that island was invaded, No. 242 followed. In September 1943 they moved again, operating from bases on the Italian mainland, sometimes with their airfields subjected to artillery fire. After a brief rest in Syria the unit moved to Corsica. About this time another CAN/RAF pilot, Flight Sergeant Ken Woodhill,[2] served with No. 242. From April 1944 onward the squadron was equipped with *Spitfire IX's*. Most of their sorties were over Italy,

---

1. In September 1944, while serving with No. 411 Squadron, Flight Lieutenant Portz destroyed three *Fw 190's* and damaged one. He was awarded the Distinguished Flying Cross on January 23rd, 1945.

2. Woodhill later transferred to the RCAF. In 1944-45, as a member of No. 401 Squadron, he destroyed one enemy aircraft, shared in the destruction of another, and shared a "damaged" claim involving a *Me 262* jet fighter.

from Genoa to Elba and as far inland as Florence and Bologna.

Anvil—the invasion of southern France—began on August 15th, 1944. No. 242 had helped pave the way by attacking German radar sites at Cap Serrat and Cap Couronne. On the 23rd No. 242 moved to Frejus, midway between Nice and Toulon. The unit had returned to France four years and two months after they had been forced to leave that country. The abrupt collapse of German resistance in southern France soon made the squadron's services redundant. On November 4th, 1944, No. 242 was disbanded.

A new No. 242 Squadron was formed at Stoney Cross, England, on November 15th, 1944. This was a transport unit flying *Wellington XVI's*, followed by *Stirlings* and then *Yorks*. The squadron maintained runs to the Middle East, India, and Singapore; in 1948-49 they participated in the Berlin Airlift. Converting to *Hastings*, No. 242 returned to transport duties between England, East Africa, and the Middle East. Finally, in April 1950, the squadron was disbanded once more.

The *Hastings* were the last conventional aircraft flown by No. 242 Squadron. In October 1959 the unit was revived again, but this time as an Air Defence Missile Squadron at Marham, Norfolk, equipped with *Bloodhound* ramjet missiles. It was disbanded on September 30th, 1964—the last chapter in the history of a famous unit.

No. 242 Squadron

Appendix A

Honours and Awards Granted to Members of No. 242 Squadron, 1939-41

Awards are listed chronologically; dates refer to official notification in the *London Gazette*; personnel were usually advised of the decoration several days in advance of the formal gazetting.

1. *Distinguished Flying Cross*—Pilot Officer William Lidstone McKnight (June 14th, 1940)

   > One day in May 1940, this officer destroyed a Messerschmitt 109 and on the following day, whilst on patrol with his squadron, he shot down three more enemy aircraft. The destruction of the last one of the three aircraft occasioned a long chase over enemy territory. On his return flight he used his remaining ammunition, and caused many casualties, in a low flying attack on a railway along which the enemy were bringing up heavy guns. Pilot Officer McKnight has shown exceptional skill and courage as a fighter pilot.

2. *Distinguished Service Order*—Squadron Leader Douglas Robert Steuart Bader (October 1st, 1940)

   > This officer has displayed gallantry and leadership of the highest order. During three recent engagements he has led his squadron with such skill and ability that thirty-three enemy aircraft have been destroyed. In the course of these engagements Squadron Leader Bader has added to his previous successes by destroying six enemy aircraft.

3. *Distinguished Flying Cross*—Flight Lieutenant George Eric Ball (October 1st, 1940)

   > This officer has destroyed five enemy aircraft. He pursued one of these at night for fifty miles before shooting it down. His excellent leadership has instilled great confidence in his flight.

4. *Bar to Distinguished Flying Cross*—Pilot Officer William Lidstone McKnight (October 8th, 1940)

   > This officer has destroyed six enemy aircraft during the last thirteen

weeks. He has proved himself to be a most efficient section leader, and has consistently given proof that he is a courageous and tenacious fighter.

5. *Distinguished Flying Cross*—Flight Lieutenant Percival Stanley Turner (October 8th, 1940)

On September 15th, 1940, Flight Lieutenant Turner succeeded in shooting down one enemy aircraft when his own aircraft was hit by a cannon shell which put it temporarily out of control. On recovery he saw and attacked a further enemy aircraft, which he destroyed, afterwards bringing his own damaged aircraft safely back to its base. This officer has personally destroyed a total of ten hostile aircraft during engagements over Dunkirk and England. He has proved himself a most courageous and capable leader, displaying coolness and initiative in the face of the enemy.

6. *Distinguished Flying Cross*—Pilot Officer Noel Karl Stansfeld (October 8th, 1940)

This officer has destroyed seven enemy aircraft during engagements over Dunkirk and England. He has exhibited excellent fighting qualities, initiative, and marked powers of leadership.

7. *Distinguished Service Cross*—Sub-Lieutenant Richard John Cork (October 18th, 1940)

For exemplary courage and coolness in successful action against enemy bombers.

Author's Note: *The decoration awarded to Cork has been the subject of some misunderstandings and myth-making. According to Paul Brickhill (Reach for the Sky, p. 228, 233-34), Cork was originally awarded a Distinguished Flying Cross. Later the Admiralty insisted that he wear a Distinguished Service Cross (the naval equivalent of the DFC). To this Bader objected, declaring that the King had given Cork a DFC, and only the King could substitute a DSC. Bader insisted that Cork wear the ribbon of the DFC as long as he flew with the Royal Air Force. When Cork returned to Fleet Air Arm duty his superiors were equally insistent that he wear the ribbon of the DSC. This story is repeated by Chris Shores,* Aces High.

The anecdote is delightful, in part because it suggests a stuffy Admiralty standing flat-footed on protocol. The diary of No. 242 Squadron and Bader's own logbook record that word had reached the unit of a DFC for Cork, and it is clear that Bader had indeed recommended him for the RAF decoration.

Nevertheless, it cannot be stated that the King had awarded a DFC to this young officer. If the London Gazette *can be taken as being the voice of the Crown, then it is obvious that Cork was awarded a Distinguished Service Cross; there is no mention in any issue of that august publication to indicate otherwise.*

The probable sequence of events was that Bader's recommendation was approved at Fighter Command Headquarters, at which point word was

*communicated to the squadron that a DFC was coming through. However,
Admiralty approval would have been sought before gazetting, and the
Admiralty would have substituted a DSC.*

*Bader evidently turned a blind eye to the official announcement, prefer-
ring to have some fun at the expense of the Senior Service. His insistence
that Cork wear the DFC ribbon while on duty with No. 242 is a matter of
record, confirmed by photographs.*

8. *Distinguished Flying Cross*—Pilot Officer John Blandford Latta
(November 8th, 1940)

> Pilot Officer Latta has destroyed eight enemy aircraft in operations over
> France and this country. On one occasion his squadron attacked a number
> of Messerschmitt 109s. This officer destroyed one and, although his own
> aircraft had been hit in the wings and tail by cannon shells, attacked and
> destroyed a second enemy aircraft. He has displayed the utmost coolness
> in the midst of fierce combat.

9. *Mentioned in Despatches*—Squadron Leader Douglas Robert
Steuart Bader (January 1st, 1941)

10. *Distinguished Flying Cross*—Squadron Leader Douglas Robert
Steuart Bader (January 7th, 1941)

> Squadron Leader Bader has continued to lead his squadron and wing
> with the utmost gallantry on all occasions. He has now destroyed a total
> of ten hostile aircraft and damaged several more.

11. *Distinguished Flying Cross*—Flying Officer Hugh Norman Tamblyn (January 7th, 1941)

> Flying Officer Tamblyn has shown the greatest keenness to engage the
> enemy and has destroyed at least five of their aircraft. He has set a splen-
> did example to the other members of his section.

12. *Distinguished Flying Cross*—Pilot Officer Denis Crowley-Milling
(April 11th, 1941)

> This officer has participated in numerous engagements against the enemy
> over a long period and has shown a fine spirit throughout. On one
> occasion he pursued a Junkers 88 out to sea and, although his aircraft
> was severely damaged by a cannon shell in the pursuit, he continued his
> attack until the enemy aircraft was on fire and disappeared into cloud 40
> miles out at sea. He displayed great courage and initiative, and has
> destroyed at least four enemy aircraft.

13. *Distinguished Flying Cross*—Flight Lieutenant Robert Davidson
Grassick (July 15th, 1941)

> This officer has been a member of the squadron since its formation. He

has displayed an indomitable spirit and has proved himself to be a first-class section leader. Flight Lieutenant Grassick has destroyed at least six enemy aircraft.

14. *Distinguished Flying Cross*—Squadron Leader Whitney Willard Straight (August 8th, 1941)

This officer has participated in many engagements against the enemy throughout which he has displayed excellent qualities of leadership and zeal. He has destroyed at least three enemy aircraft, one of which he shot down at night.

15. *Distinguished Flying Cross*—Pilot Officer Nigel Leslie Digby Kemp (October 7th, 1941)

Since May this officer has participated in twenty-nine operational sorties, fifteen of which have been directed against enemy shipping. Throughout, Pilot Officer Kemp has displayed great courage and initiative, combined with a fine fighting spirit. On one occasion he machine-gunned German troops on the beach at Fort Phillips, causing casualties. On another occasion, when flying alone over the Channel, he attacked a fast enemy launch, from which he had been fired at, silenced its guns, and stopped the vessel. Pilot Officer Kemp has contributed materially to the successes achieved by his unit against enemy shipping.

16. *Distinguished Flying Cross*—Pilot Officer John Philip McKechnie (October 7th, 1941, with effect from August 28th, 1941)

This officer has led his section on numerous important daylight attacks on enemy shipping. Displaying great leadership and determination, often in the face of heavy fire from ships and ground defences, Pilot Officer McKechnie has contributed materially to the successes achieved. He has also participated in many fighter sweeps and bomber escorts. On one occasion Pilot Officer McKechnie was instrumental in guiding a rescue launch to one of our pilots, who had been forced to descend into the sea in mid-Channel. Throughout he has shown a high degree of skill and courage.

Appendix B

Aircrew Personnel of No. 242 Squadron, 1939-41

Canadians listed in block capitals.

Rank and Name	Reported	Disposal
S/L F.M GOBEIL (RCAF)	1.11.39	Transferred 24.6.40
F/L D.R. MILLER	3.11.39	Posted 9.6.40
F/L J.L. SULLIVAN	3.11.39	Killed in action 14.5.40
F/O J.W. GRAAFSTRA	5.11.39	Killed in action 23.5.40
P/O R.D. GRASSICK	5.11.39	Posted 28.9.41
P/O M.K. BROWN	6.11.39	Wounded 18.5.40
		Rejoined 13.7.40
		Killed accidentally 21.2.41
F/O L.E. CHAMBERS	6.11.39	Prisoner of War, 18.5.40
P/O A.H. DEACON	6.11.39	Prisoner of War, 28.5.40
P/O R.L. HILL	6.11.39	Killed in action 24.5.40
P/O D.F. JONES	6.11.39	Killed in action 28.5.40
P/O W.L. McKNIGHT	6.11.39	Killed in action 12.1.41
P/O D.G. MacQUEEN	6.11.39	Killed in action 9.6.40
P/O G.A. MADORE	6.11.39	Killed in action 23.5.40
P/O J.W. MITCHELL	6.11.39	Killed in action 24.5.40
P/O H.L. NICCOLLS	6.11.39	Killed accidentally 3.3.40
P/O J.B. SMILEY	6.11.39	Prisoner of War, 23.5.40
P/O R.H. WIENS	6.11.39	Wounded 18.5.40
P/O J.B. LATTA	6.11.39	Killed in action 12.1.41
F/O R. COE	7.11.39	Killed accidentally 10.1.40
P/O J.F. HOWITT	20.11.39	Injured accidentally 29.5.40
P/O P.S. TURNER	20.11.39	Posted 13.4.41
P/O W.A. WATERTON	20.11.39	Posted 20.8.40
P/O J. BENZIE	3.2.40	Wounded 23.5.40
		Rejoined 11.7.40
		Killed in action 7.9.40
P/O N.K. STANSFELD	3.2.40	Posted 29.9.40
P/O G.M. STEWART	28.5.40	Killed in action 31.5.40
F/L G.H. Plinston	28.5.40	Posted 30.6.40

P/O H.E. Horne	2.6.40	Posted 12.6.40
P/O N.N. CAMPBELL	3.6.40	Killed in action 17.10.40
P/O A.E. Eckford	3.6.40	Posted 29.7.40
P/O R. Atkinson	6.40	Posted 10.8.40
Sgt. E. Richardson	6.40	Posted 18.7.40
P/O C.R. Bush (New Zealand)	6.6.40	No record after 15.11.40
P/O D. Crowley-Milling	6.6.40	Posted 13.6.41
S/L D.R.S. Bader	24.6.40	Posted 16.3.41
F/L G.E. Ball	24.6.40	Posted 29.1.41
Sgt. A.D. Meredith	6.40	Posted 9.8.40
Sgt. G.W. Brimble	6.40	Posted 6.11.40
Sgt. J.F. Armitage	6.40	No record after August 1940
Sgt. Terras	6.40	No further record
Sgt. J.A. Porter	6.40	Posted 10.8.40
Sub-Lt. R.J. Cork	1.7.40	No record after 23.11.40
Sub-Lt. R.E. Gardner	1.7.40	No record after 28.11.40
Midshipman R.J. Patterson	1.7.40	Killed accidentally 20.8.40
F/L G.F. Powell-Sheddon	7.40	Wounded 15.9.40
		Posted 22.11.40
P/O N. HART	18.7.40	Killed in action 5.11.40
Sgt. R.V. Lonsdale	20.7.40	No record after 12.10.40
F/O G.P. CHRISTIE	21.7.40	Posted 3.9.40
P/O H.N. TAMBLYN	5.8.40	Killed in action 3.4.41
F/O J.G. CAVE	11.8.40	Posted 3.10.40
P/O K.M. SCLANDERS	26.8.40	Killed in action 9.9.40
P/O L.E. CRYDERMAN	31.8.40	To No. 5 OTU, 3.9.40
		Rejoined 26.9.40
		Killed in action 8.2.41
P/O R.H. DIBNAH	21.9.40	Posted 30.12.40
P/O M.G. Homer	21.9.40	Killed in action 27.9.40
Sgt. J.E. Saville	21.9.40	No record after 12.10.40
P/O B.A. Rogers	28.9.40	Killed in action 17.6.41
P/O M.P. Warsham	17.10.40	Posted 6.11.40
P/O J.G.P. Millard	17.10.40	Posted 3.11.40
P/O C.B. Savory	18.10.40	No further record
P/O H.L.D. Kemp	18.10.40	Still with squadron, 10.41
P/O J.J. Robinson	24.10.40	No further record
P/O A.W. SMITH	4.11.40	Killed accidentally 28.3.41
F/O E.O. Lang	6.11.40	Killed accidentally 20.4.41
Sgt. L.R. Truman	7.11.40	Posted 17.12.40
P/O N.D. EDMOND	22.11.40	Killed accidentally 20.4.41
F/O L.E. PRICE (RCAF)	28.11.40	Posted 29.1.41
P/O D.J. McKENNA (RCAF)	28.11.40	Posted 29.1.41

P/O J.A. DESCHAMPS	4.12.40	Posted 30.12.40
P/O C.I.R. ARTHUR	12.12.40	Posted 23.5.41
P/O F. Surma (Polish)	17.12.40	Posted 13.3.41
P/O H. Szczesny (Polish)	17.12.40	No further record
Sgt. A.J. Vaughan	4.1.41	Killed accidentally 26.4.41
Sgt. J.R. Pollard	29.1.41	Posted 11.3.41
Sgt. E.A. Redfern	29.1.41	Missing 17.8.41
P/O K.M. Hicks (Australian)	18.2.41	Missing 17.8.41
P/O J.P. McKechnie (Australian)	18.2.41	Prisoner of War, 19.8.41
P/O D.K. Oak-Rhind (Australian)	18.2.41	Missing 21.5.41
Sgt. Jessop	2.41	Posted 11.3.41
Sgt. E.H.C. Kee	2.41	Still with squadron, 10.41
S/L W.P.F. Treacy	14.3.41	Killed accidentally 20.4.41
Sgt. Etchells	14.3.41	No record after April 1941
F/L M.J. Loudon	4.41	Posted 23.7.41
Sgt. David	4.41	Killed accidentally 23.4.41
P/O J. Byrks (Czech)	14.4.41	Prisoner of War, 17.6.41
S/L W.W. Straight	23.4.41	Missing 31.7.41
P/O F.E. Fayolle (French)	26.4.41	Posted 14.10.41
P/O F.H. de Labouchere (French)	26.4.41	Posted 13.9.41
P/O S. Skalski	26.4.41	Posted 7.6.41
P/O T. Kozak	26.4.41	Killed accidentally 14.6.41
F/L P. de Scitivaux (French)	26.4.41	Posted 19.9.41
Sgt. Hall	5.5.41	Still with squadron, 10.41
Sgt. M.G.A.C. CASGRAIN (RCAF)	5.5.41	Killed in action 1.8.41
Sgt. G.A. PROSSER (RCAF)	5.5.41	Killed in action 27.7.41
Sgt. Lillywhite	13.5.41	Posted 21.6.41
Sgt. Westcott	13.6.41	Posted 19.6.41
Captain O. Bull (Norwegian)	2.6.41	Posted 8.8.41
Lt. E. Hagen (Norwegian)	2.6.41	Posted 8.8.41
Lt. H.O. Mehre (Norwegian)	2.6.41	Posted 8.8.41
F/L B. Duperier (French)	6.41	Posted 13.9.41
S/L E.T. Smith (supernumerary)	28.4.41	Prisoner of War, 17.6.41
P/O R.F. Hamlyn	13.6.41	Posted 15.10.41
F/L J.E.F. Demozay (French)	21.6.41	Posted 29.6.41
Sgt. Shaw	24.6.41	Posted 30.6.41
Sgt. May	24.6.41	Posted 3.7.41
P/O T.N. McNamara	3.7.41	Still with squadron, 10.41
P/O J. de Pelleport (French)	17.7.41	Missing 10.8.41
F/L V.G. Daw	17.7.41	Posted 8.8.41
S/L W.G. Wells	1.8.41	Still with squadron, 10.41
P/O H. Quilliam	5.8.41	Missing in action 26.8.41
P/O N.J. Lezemore	5.8.41	Killed accidentally 29.8.41

Sgt. Welling	6.8.41	No further record
F/O Andrews	7.8.41	Still with squadron, 10.41
Sgt. Sands (Australian)	8.41	Posted 27.9.41
Sgt. Manby	8.41	Posted 2.10.41
P/O C.E. SLUGGETT	23.8.41	Posted to Malta, 1942
Sgt. H. HALE (RCAF)	23.8.41	Posted to Western Desert, 1942
Sgt. R.V. HARVEY (RCAF)	23.8.41	Posted to Malta, 1942
P/O J.G.F. Booth	28.8.41	Posted 27.9.41
Sgt. Reilly	4.9.41	Missing 10.9.41
P/O Mize (American)	4.9.41	Posted 13.10.41
P/O Reed (American)	4.9.41	Posted 13.10.41
Sgt. Oldham	9.9.41	Posted 11.9.41
Sgt. Carroll	9.9.41	Posted 11.9.41
P/O Hay	22.9.41	Still with squadron, 10.41
P/O Blanchard	22.9.41	Still with squadron, 10.41
P/O C.R. Morrison-Jones	22.9.41	Still with squadron, 10.41
P/O J. Coignard (French)	22.9.41	Posted 10.10.41
Sgt. Mulley	22.9.41	Still with squadron, 10.41
Sgt. Mailfert (French)	22.9.41	Posted 10.10.41
Sgt. Lawes	22.9.41	Still with squadron, 10.41
Sgt. Jones	22.9.41	Still with squadron, 10.41
Sgt. Massey	22.9.41	Still with squadron, 10.41
Sgt. HALLIWELL (RCAF)	22.9.41	Posted 27.9.41
Sgt. CASE (RCAF)	22.9.41	Posted 27.9.41
Sgt. Spencer	22.9.41	Posted 27.9.41
F/O H.W. Eliot	24.9.41	Posted 10.10.41
P/O Tew	10.41	Still with squadron, 10.41
P/O Addy	10.41	
Sgt. Gray	7.10.41	
Sgt. Goodwin	9.10.41	
F/O Egerton	17.10.41	
P/O Brown	20.10.41	
Sgt. Collins (Australian)	22.10.41	
Sgt. J.L. Boyd (Australian)	22.10.41	Posted to Malta, 1942
Sgt. Neale	22.10.41	
Sgt. Isdale	22.10.41	
Sgt. Gardiner	28.10.41	

Appendix C

Canadian Groundcrew Serving in No. 242 Squadron, 1940-41

No. 242 Squadron's Operational Record Book did not record groundcrew movements, and other documents are vague or incomplete in listing Canadian tradesmen. The following names are drawn from several sources.

In February 1940 the RAF compiled a list of Canadians serving in that force. This was in response to requests from RCAF and Canadian Red Cross authorities; it gave service numbers, ranks, names, and the addresses of next of kin; it did not identify units with which the men were serving. In any case, it was clearly drawn up before No. 242 began receiving substantial numbers of Canadian tradesmen, although it did indicate the size of the pool from which they might be secured. This was placed on RCAF Overseas Headquarters file 22/2/1, *Records of Canadians in RAF*; it is now held by the Directorate of History, Canadian Forces Headquarters (Reference 181.005 Docket 270).

Another list of CAN/RAF airmen was compiled in May 1941 and placed on RCAF Overseas Headquarters file C.23, Nominal Roll, *Canadians in RAF*, now with the Directorate of History (Reference 181.005 Docket 271). This was similar to the earlier list, but noted trades of the men and the units with which they were then serving. Additional lists made their way into RCAF Overseas Headquarters file 22-15, *Canadians in RAF*, and thence to the Directorate of History (Reference 181.005, Dockets 1094 to 1096 and 1235). All these documents failed to state what criteria were used to define "Canadian", and some people may have had very tentative claims to being so when we note that in several cases the immediate next of kin (including parents) were themselves in the United Kingdom.

The recollections of Albert Taylor have been helpful in identifying several airmen as serving with No. 242 Squadron, particularly those who joined and departed between the time' that the two RAF lists were compiled. Nevertheless, there remain several anomalies and contradictions in the record; these will be apparent as one combs the list.

568825	Corporal R.G. Aedy Fitter 2E Father in U.K.	Listed as a Canadian with No. 242, May 1941. Later commissioned in Technical Branch (Enginner), April 15th, 1943.
649169	AC.1 J.B. Bailey Aircraft Hand/General Duties Wife in U.K.	Listed as a Canadian with No. 242, May 1941.
654698	AC.1 J.E.R. Baines Fitter Mechanic E Victoria, B.C.	With No. 242, May 1941.
610348	Corporal N.A. Barlow Fitter 2E Carsland, Alberta	In France, June 1940. MiD for services. Still with No. 242, May 1941. Later trained as pilot.
625780	(Rank?) C.L. Batten Trade unknown Father in U.K.; variously identified as being from Victoria or Vancouver.	Identified by A.W. Taylor as being with No. 242; not fully described in RAF lists.
541245	Corporal F.S. Batty Metal Rigger Toronto, Ontario	With No. 2 Bombing and Gunnery School, May 1941, but had been in No. 242 before then.
906582	AC.1 B.B. Bennett Aircraft Hand/General Duties Father in U.K.; believed to have been in Victoria before war.	Still with No. 242, May 1941.
633673	AC.1 L.J. Benson Fitter 2E Nanaimo, British Columbia	With No. 242, 1940-41, but gone to No. 13 MU by May 1941. Later trained as pilot.
904956	AC.1 A.J.M. Bone Fitter 2E Vancouver, British Columbia	Still with No. 242, May 1941.
545251	Corporal R.J. Bottomly Armourer Saskatoon, Saskatchewan	With No. 242, 1940-41, but with No. 71 Squadron by May 1941.

536800	Corporal J.A. Breadner Metal Rigger Niagara-on-the-Lake, Ontario	With No. 242, 1940-41, but gone to No. 1 AACU by May 1941.
645294	LAC E.T. Cameron Fitter Mechanic E New Glasgow, Nova Scotia	No. 242, January 12th, 1940 to August 1941; in France, May 1940. Remustered to pilot, commissioned May 25th, 1944.
571595	Corporal P. Clifford Fitter 2A Winnipeg, Manitoba	Listed as Canadian with No. 242, May 1941. Later trained as pilot, commissioned February 26th, 1943.
912726	AC.1 R.T. Coupland Aircraft Hand/General Duties Winnipeg, Manitoba	Still in No. 242, May 1941.
628629	LAC F.C. Curle Fitter Mechanic E Cranbrook, British Columbia	Still in No. 242, May 1941.
?	Sergeant "Jack" Cowling Trade unknown American	Identified by Hitchins and Taylor; no details available.
639280	LAC A.E. Deloume Fitter Mechanic E Cottle Hill, British Columbia	In France, June 1940. Later posted to Rhodesia (where stationed, May 1941). Later remustered to aircrew.
570730	Corporal M.B. Dunn Fitter 2 Vancouver, British Columbia	Still in No. 242, May 1941.
536189	Corporal F.C. Dyer Armourer Vancouver, British Columbia	In France, June 1940. Still in No. 242, May 1941.
616537	LAC T.M. Einboden Fitter 2A Lansing, Ontario	To France, June 1940. As of May 1941 with Station Cosford. Commissioned October 10th, 1942 in Technical Branch (Engineer).
546842	LAC M.H. Fallis	Listed as Canadian with No.

	Wireless Operator Father in U.K.	242, May 1941.
623336	LAC K. Fisher Fitter Mechanic E Victoria, British Columbia	To France, June 1940. Still in No. 242, May 1941.
637109	AC.1 H.L. Galbraith Armourer Vancouver, British Columbia	To France, June 1940. Still in No. 242, May 1941.
637112	LAC T.F. Galbraith Wireless Operator Vancouver, British Columbia	To France, May 1940. Still in No. 242, May 1941. Remustered to pilot, com- missioned October 1941.
645733	LAC C.T. Gibbons Fitter Mechanic E Nanaimo, British Columbia	To France, May 1940. Still in No. 242, May 1941.
617556	LAC J.E. Girling Aircraft Hand/General Duties Saskatoon, Saskatchewan	To France, June 1940. As of May 1941 was at Station Lerwick.
614198	AC.1 R. Goatley Fitter 2A Tillsonberg, Ontario	In Canada as of May 1941.
542422	AC.1 L. Greenburgh Fitter Mechanic 2 Winnipeg, Manitoba	In No. 242, March 20th to April 10th, 1940: Later trained as pilot, commis- sioned September 25th, 1942. Awarded DFC and Bar, 1944.
?	(Rank?) A.C. Griffin Trade unknown Residence unknown	Name supplied by A.W. Taylor; not on RAF lists of Canadians in that force.
620894	AC.1 J. Guest Aircraft Hand/General Duties Sister in U.K.	With No. 242 Squadron, 1940. At No. 9 STT as of May 1941. Commissioned October 7th, 1943 in Administration Branch.
526190	Corporal M.F. Hayes Metal Rigger	In No. 242 Squadron, 1941. As of May 1941, with

Medicine Hat, Alberta   Station Kirkham.

908012   AC.1 L. Holtum
Aircraft Hand/General Duties
Victoria, British Columbia

In France, June 1940. Still in No. 242, May 1941.

623543   LAC A. Hughes
Fitter 2A
Winnipeg, Manitoba

No. 242 Squadron, 1940-41. With No. 115 Squadron as of May 1941.

546802   LAC K. Hughes
Fitter 2A
Victoria, British Columbia

No. 242 Squadron, 1940-41. With No. 43 Squadron as of May 1941.

648769   AC.1 H.S. Jeffs
Wireless Operator
Vancouver, British Columbia

To France, June 1940. Still in No. 242, May 1941. Remustered to Navigator, commissioned November 12th, 1943.

572421   Corporal B.J. Jones
Fitter 2E
Toronto, Ontario

In No. 242, 1940. With No. 2 BATF as of May 1941.

566617   Corporal T. Knight
Fitter 2
Vancouver, British Columbia

Recorded in RAF lists as being with No. 242, May 1941.

621535   Corporal C.F. Langley
Clerk/General Duties
Wife and sister in U.K.; believed to be from Vancouver, British Columbia.

Still in No. 242, May 1941.

634971   AC.1 F.D. Leason
Fitter 2A
Victoria, British Columbia

With No. 242, 1940. At No. 13 MU as of May 1941.

568360   Corporal A. Long
Fitter 2
Brother in UK; believed to be from Vancouver, British Columbia.

With No. 242, 1940. Still with unit as of May 1941.

613408   Sergeant R.L. McDonald
Fitter/Armourer
Toronto, Ontario

Joined No. 242, 1940. Still with unit, May 1941.

651714   LAC A. McDougall

With No. 242, 1940. In

	Fitter Mechanic A Ottawa, Ontario	Rhodesia as of May 1941.
628275	LAC R.J. McGregor Aircraft Hand/General Duties Mother in U.K.; believed to be from Victoria, British Columbia.	Joined No. 242, 1940. Still with unit as of May 1941.
629374	AC.2 P.C. Marshall Fitter 2E Penhurst, Ontario	With No. 242, 1940. At Station Ford as of May 1941. Later remustered to Flight Engineer; commis- sioned February 25th, 1944.
616974	LAC A.A. Martin Electrician Edmonton, Alberta	In France, May 1940. Still with unit, May 1941.
643874	LAC C.W. Martindale Fitter Mechanic E Vancouver, British Columbia	No. 242 Squadron, January 1940 to May 1941; France, June 1940. Later remustered to Flight Engineer; commis- sioned September 18th, 1944.
629222	LAC R.A. Metcalfe Armourer Winnipeg, Manitoba	No. 242 association mentioned by A.W. Taylor; not on RAF lists of CAN/ RAF personnel. France, June 1940.
?	(Rank?) R. Mitchell Trade unknown Residence unknown	Name provided by A.W. Taylor; in France June 1940.
546185	AC.1 R. Myhre Fitter/Armourer Father in U.K.; believed to be from Victoria, British Columbia	No. 242 Squadron, 1940. With No. 86 MU as of May 1941.
629456	AC.1 T.H. Nelson Aircraft Hand/General Duties Montreal, Quebec	With No. 95 Squadron by May 1941.
612280	AC.1 S.G. Norris Fitter 2A	With No. 242, 1940-41. Later remustered to Naviga-

Toronto, Ontario

tor; commissioned January 2nd, 1943.

1354639   AC.1 A. Pierce
Aircraft Hand/General Duties
Kingston, Nova Scotia

With No. 242, May 1941.

634419   AC.1 A. Ralph
Fitter 2A
Toronto, Ontario

With No. 242, 1940; en route to Aden as of May 1941.

616612   LAC D. Rice
Aircraft Hand/General Duties
Verdun, Quebec

In France, June 1940. Still with unit as of May 1941.

545472   LAC G.A. Robbins
Fitter 2A
Windsor, Ontario

No. 242 association provided by A.W. Taylor.

549244   Corporal G.A. Rolfe
Fitter 2E
Wolseley, Saskatchewan

With No. 242, May 1941.

639129   AC.1 R.E. Ryerson
Aircraft Hand/General Duties
Hamilton, Ontario

With No. 242, May 1941.

573678   LAC R.E. Sabourin
Fitter/Armourer
Salmon Arm, British Columbia

No. 242, March 1940 to September 1941; France in June 1940.

629956   LAC D. Seaburn
Aircraft Hand/General Duties
Birdsall, Ontario

With No. 242, May 1941.

624776   LAC W. Shields
Fitter Mechanic A
Brother in U.K.

Listed in May 1941 as a Canadian with No. 242.

624064   LAC G.W. Sleigh
Fitter Mechanic E
Father in U.K.; believed to be from Vancouver, British Columbia

In France, May 1940. With No. 222 Squadron as of May 1941. Later Navigator, commissioned September 20th, 1944.

621313   LAC H.N. Smith
Fitter 2E

With No. 242, May 1941.

New Westminster, British Columbia

641760	AC.1 A. Sowerby Fitter Mechanic New Westminster, British Columbia	In unit, June 1940.
646808	LAC D.R. Stephens Fitter Mechanic E Aunt in U.K.; believed to be from Duncan, British Columbia	In France, May 1940. Still with unit in May 1941. Remustered to pilot, commissioned April 25th, 1942.
651717	AC.1 R. Stokes Fitter Mechanic A Toronto, Ontario	No. 242, 1940; at Station Cosford as of May 1941.
637977	AC.1 S.G. Stopford Wireless Operator North Vancouver, British Columbia	Still with No. 242, May 1941.
567889	Corporal L.H. Stopforth Fitter 2 Moose Jaw, Saskatchewan	In No. 242, 1940-41; still with unit, May 1941. Commissioned in Technical Engineering Branch October 7th, 1941.
540005	(Rank?) A. Southall Trade unknown Victoria, British Columbia	In France, June 1940 (A.W. Taylor).
1288621	AC.1 V.E. Syrett Trade unknown Victoria, British Columbia	No. 242 connection supplied by A.W. Taylor; POW in Asia; died in captivity.
611994	AC.1 L.L. Taverner Armourer Winnipeg, Manitoba	In France, June 1940. Still with unit, May 1941.
616501	LAC A.W. Taylor Fitter Mechanic E Victoria, British Columbia	In No. 242, 1940-41; in France, May and June 1940. Posted out, late spring 1941. Remustered to pilot; commissioned April 10th, 1944.
616798	LAC G. Tyler Fitter Mechanic E	No. 242, 1940. With No. 212 Squadron in May 1941.

Sudbury, Ontario

628599	LAC A.G. Tyrell Fitter Mechanic E Harey, British Columbia and Togo, Saskatchewan	No. 242, 1940; with No. 7 STT as of May 1941.
534532	Corporal C. Tyrell Fitter/Armourer Sault Ste. Marie, Ontario	No. 242, 1940; with No. 239 Squadron as of May 1941.
633110	AC.1 J.H.C. Underwood Fitter 2E Rochford Bridge, Alberta	No. 242, 1940; with No. 2 FTS as of May 1941.
?	LAC S. Walton Trade unknown Seattle, Washington	Name supplied by A.W. Taylor; not on CAN/RAF lists.
618423	LAC J. Wheeler Aircraft Hand/General Duties Father in U.K.	Listed as a Canadian with No. 242, May 1941.
619107	AC.1 H.J. Whelan Clerk Westmount, Quebec	No. 242 association supplied by A.W. Taylor.
628613	LAC J. Williams Fitter 2A Aunt in U.K.; believed to be from Vancouver, British Columbia	To France, June 1940. With No. 8 BATU as of May 1941. Later remustered to Navigator; commissioned March 23rd, 1943.
612201	LAC G.B. Wilson Aircraft Hand/General Duties Saint John, New Brunswick	With No. 242, May 1941.
535036	AC.1 F.A. Woodley-Page Fitter 2A Montreal, Quebec	With No. 242, May 1941.
629893	Corporal W. Yeardye Armourer Wife and mother in U.K.	With No. 242, May 1941. POW in Asia, 1942.

Appendix D

Representative Aircraft Flown by No. 242 Squadron

Bristol *Blenheim I*

L1168	Recorded in Miller logbook, November 1939.
L1521	Later transferred to No. 64 Squadron.
L1522	Later transferred to No. 64 Squadron.
L1523	Later transferred to No. 64 Squadron.
L1524	Later transferred to No. 64 Squadron.
L6789	Later transferred to No. 235 Squadron.
L6790	Later transferred to No. 235 Squadron.
L6791	Later transferred to No. 64 Squadron.
L6792	Later transferred to No. 235 Squadron.
K7122	From Station Wyton. Later transferred to No. 235 Squadron.

Fairey *Battle I*

L5014	From No. 235 Squadron. Later transferred to No. 3 BGS.
L5133	From No. 235 Squadron. Later transferred to No. 141 Squadron.
L5406	From No. 235 Squadron. Later transferred to No. 141 Squadron.

Miles *Magister*

L8284	Recorded in Miller logbook, November. Apparently exchanged for P2441.
N3952	From No. 53 Squadron. Crashed in forced landing, November 19th, 1940. Pilot Officer McKnight baled out, uninjured.
P2441	Later transferred to No. 219 Squadron.
P2503	From No. 66 Squadron. Later transferred to No. 6 FIS.

North American *Harvard*

P5865	From No. 609 Squadron. Later returned to that unit.

Hawker *Hurricane*

L1572	LE-F. From No. 32 Squadron. Later transferred to No. 501 Squadron.
L1584	From No. 111 Squadron. Later transferred to No. 56 Squadron.
L1595	From No. 504 Squadron. Later transferred to No. 249 Squadron.

L1638	From No. 504 Squadron. Later transferred to No. 56 OTU.
L1654	From No. 151 Squadron. Later transferred to No. 6 OTU.
L1665	From No. 32 Squadron. Missing, May 18th, 1940.
L1666	From No. 32 Squadron. Later transferred to No. 253 Squadron.
L1746	From No. 17 Squadron. Missing, May 28th, 1940. Pilot Officer D.F. Jones missing.
L1747	From No. 151 Squadron. Later transferred to No. 32 Squadron.
L1748	From No. 151 Squadron. Later transferred to No. 56 Squadron.
L1749	From No. 151 Squadron. Missing in France, May 1940.
L1756	LE-U. From No. 151 Squadron. Crashed on takeoff, Manston, May 29th, 1940. Pilot Officer J.F. Howitt injured.
L1757	From No. 151 Squadron. Later transferred to No. 1 Squadron.
L1766	From No. 151 Squadron. Later transferred to No. 73 Squadron.
L1922	From No. 504 Squadron. Missing, May 1940.
L1948	From No. 504 Squadron. James J. Halley, *Royal Air Force Aircraft L1000-L9999*, states it was with No. 242 and lost on June 1st, 1940. No squadron casualty occurred on that date; the machine may have been transferred or loaned to another unit with which it went missing.
L1972	LE-G. From No. 32 Squadron. Later transferred to No. 56 Squadron.
L1981	From No. 56 Squadron. Later transferred to No. 73 Squadron.
L1983	From No. 56 Squadron. Later returned to No. 56 Squadron.
L1992	From No. 56 Squadron. Later returned to No. 56 Squadron.
L2002	From No. 56 Squadron. Crashed during night flying training, March 3rd, 1940. Pilot Officer H.L. Niccolls killed.
L2003	LE-A. From No. 56 Squadron. Later transferred to No. 615 Squadron.
L2004	From No. 56 Squadron. James J. Halley, *ibid.*, states that it was lost on June 1st, 1940, with No. 242. No casualties recorded on this day; the machine may have been transferred or loaned to another unit, with which it was lost.
L2039	From No. 501 Squadron. Later transferred to No. 73 Squadron.
L2087	From No. 151 Squadron. Later transferred to No. 52 OTU.
L2090	From No. 29 Squadron. Crashed, September 30th, 1940 (Halley, *ibid.*); incident not traced in squadron records.
L2064	Recorded in Howitt logbook, February 1940.
L2072	Recorded in Howitt logbook, February 1940.
N2320	LE-H. From No. 56 Squadron. Lost in France, May 1940.
N2338	Later transferred to No. 7 OTU.
N2341	Later transferred to No. 7 OTU.
N2342	Later transferred to No. 32 Squadron.
N2343	Later transferred to No. 6 OTU.

N2344	Later transferred to No. 56 Squadron.
N2345	Later transferred to No. 46 Squadron.
N2357	Recorded in Howitt logbook, February 1940.
N2365	Recorded in Howitt logbook, February 1940.
N2381	From No. 1 Squadron. Burnt on evacuation from Nantes, June 18th, 1940.
N2424	From No. 253 Squadron. Halley, *Royal Air Force Aircraft N1000-N9999*, records it as being lost on June 1st, 1940. No unit casualties occurred this day. Possibly lost with another unit.
N2476	From No. 310 Squadron. Spun in and crashed, February 21st, 1941. Pilot Officer M.K. Brown killed.
N2651	From No. 151 Squadron. Shot down, May 28th, 1940. Pilot Officer A.H. Deacon taken prisoner.
P2550	From No. 56 Squadron. Shot down near Cambrai, May 23rd, 1940. Pilot Officer J. Benzie wounded.
P2730	Shot down near Cambrai, May 23rd, 1940. Pilot Officer G.A. Madore killed.
P2732	Shot down near Dunkirk, May 31st, 1940. Pilot Officer G.M. Stewart killed.
P2767	Shot down in France, June 9th, 1940. Pilot Officer D.G. MacQueen killed.
P2769	LE-Q. From No. 249 Squadron. Later transferred to No. 79 Squadron.
P2806	From No. 85 Squadron. Shot down, November 5th, 1940. Pilot Officer N. Hart killed.
P2809	Shot down, May 23rd, 1940. Pilot Officer J.W. Graafstra killed.
P2831	Abandoned near London, September 9th, 1940. Sergeant L.E.V.H. Lonsdale baled out, uninjured.
P2854	Later transferred to No. 32 Squadron.
P2878	Later transferred to No. 615 Squadron.
P2884	From No. 111 Squadron. Halley, *Royal Air Force Aircraft P1000-P9999*, records it being lost with No. 242 on May 31st, 1940. No unit casualty can be traced to this particular machine; it may possibly have been flown by Flight Lieutenant Plinston, whose aircraft was much shot about that day. Winston G. Ramsey, *The Battle of Britain, Then and Now*, lists it as being shot down on September 15th, 1940, Flight Lieutenant G.F. Powell-Sheddon injured.
P2961	LE-A. Regularly flown by Pilot Officer W.L. McKnight during the Battle of Britain, and lost with him on January 12th, 1941.
P2962	From No. 73 Squadron. Shot down on September 7th, 1940. Pilot Officer J. Benzie killed.
P2965	LE-X.

P2967	Shot down, September 27th, 1940. Pilot Officer M.G. Homer killed.
P2976	Crashed in sea, August 20th, 1940. Midshipman P.J. Patterson killed.
P3034	From No. 73 Squadron. Later transferred to No. 111 Squadron.
P3054	LE-N.
P3061	Damaged, September 7th, 1940, while piloted by Squadron Leader D.R.S. Bader.
P3087	Shot down, September 9th, 1940. Pilot Officer K.M. Sclanders killed.
P3088	LE-L. Crashed by Pilot Officer Grassick, July 11th, 1940. Later transferred to No. 249 Squadron.
P3089	Later transferred to No. 303 Squadron.
P3090	Struck off RAF strength, April 1941.
P3207	Damaged, September 7th, 1940, while piloted by Sub-Lieutenant R.J. Cork. Damaged, October 17th, 1940, while flown by Pilot Officer M.K. Brown. Later transferred to No. 55 OTU.
P3218	Later transferred to No. 52 OTU.
P32661	Lost through collision, May 24th, 1940. Pilot Officer R.L. Hill killed.
P3268	Later transferred to No. 7 OTU.
P3271	Halley, *ibid.*, records it being lost with No. 242 Squadron on July 25th, 1940. No casualty in unit on this date, and not mentioned in other source material.
P3272	Lost through collision, May 24th, 1940. Pilot Officer J.W. Mitchell lost.
P3372	Shot down near Cambrai, May 23rd, 1940. Pilot Officer J.W. Smiley taken prisoner.
P3467	From No. 85 Squadron. Later transferred to No. 55 OTU.
P3485	LE-Y. Flown by Pilot Officer Turner in combat of September 9th, 1940. Later transferred to Station Speke.
P3515	From No. 111 Squadron. Later transferred to No. 257 Squadron.
P3683	Burnt on evacuation from Nantes, June 18th, 1940.
P3683	Later transferred to No. 1 Squadron.
P3715	LE-M. Damaged, September 7th, 1940, while flown by Pilot Officer D. Crowley-Milling.
P3779	Burnt on evacuation from Nantes, June 18th, 1940.
P3813	Later transferred to No. 151 Squadron.
P3814	Later transferred to No. 303 Squadron.
P3815	Later transferred to No. 501 Squadron.
P3864	LE-U. Later transferred to Royal Aeronautical Establishment.
R4115	LE-X. Flown by Pilot Officer H.N. Tamblyn on September 9th, 1940.

V6575	Shot down, October 17th, 1940. Pilot Officer N.N. Campbell killed.
V6576	Force-landed after combat, September 15th, 1940, while piloted by Flight Lieutenant G.E. Ball. Repaired, and force-landed again after combat of September 27th, 1940, again with Ball.
V6675	LE-V.
V6913	LE-G.
V7203	LE-T. Lost, January 12th, 1941. Flying Officer J.B. Latta killed.
V7467	LE-D. Regularly flown by Squadron Leader D.R.S. Bader.

Hawker Hurricane II

Z2348	LE-H. Recorded in Mehre logbook. Mk.IIa.
Z2461	Recorded in Mehre logbook. Mk.IIa.
Z2513	LE-A. Mk.IIa.
Z2582	Mk.IIa.
Z2588	LE-S. Mk.IIa.
Z2632	LE-A. Mk.IIb.
Z2633	LE-I. Recorded in Mehre logbook. Mk.IIb.
Z2742	LE-V. Recorded in Mehre logbook. Mk.IIa.
Z2747	Mk.IIa.
Z2906	Recorded in Mehre logbook. Mk.IIa.
Z3075	Recorded in Mehre logbook. Mk.IIc.
Z3076	Recorded in Mehre logbook. Mk.IIc.
Z3089	LE-A. Recorded in Mehre logbook. Mk.IIa.
Z3156	Recorded in Mehre logbook. Mk.IIb.
Z3246	Recorded in Mehre logbook. Mk.IIc.
Z3255	Recorded in Mehre logbook. Mk.IIc.
Z3504	Mk.IIc.
Z3519	LE-X. Illustrated in *La Vielle Equipe*.
Z3556	LE-F. Illustrated in *La Vielle Equipe*.
Z5451	Mk.IIa.
BD787	Mk.IIc.
BD831	Mk.IIc.
BD832	Mk.IIc.
BD875	Mk.IIc.

Hawker Hurricane

With the exception of the brief opening interlude on *Blenheim I's*, the Hawker *Hurricane* was to be No. 242's mount for the first two years of the squadron's existence. The most numerous RAF fighter in the Battle of Britain (30 squadrons as opposed to nineteen of *Spitfires*), the *Hurricane* nevertheless lacked the glamour of its more graceful partner. Among pilots, the *Hurricane* was respected but not particularly loved. Whereas *Spitfire* and *Bf 109* pilots might dispute the relative merits of their respective aircraft, it is fair to say that *Hurricane* pilots would much rather have been flying *Spitfires*. In almost all aspects save diving speed and turning radius, the *Spitfire* was superior; it was faster, climbed better, turned more quickly, and rolled more briskly. Nevertheless, the *Hurricane* had an exceptionally steady gun platform, and this quality, combined with its ability to withstand battle damage, made it an effective combat aircraft in the hands of competent flyers. The *Hurricane* was also kinder to new pilots. Its sturdy undercarriage was more tolerant of rough fields and novice hands than the fragile oleo legs of the *Spitfire*. Yet the type had reached the peak of its development by late 1940, unlike the *Spitfire* which was just beginning its long career of modification. Early in 1941 the appearance of the *Bf 109F* spelled the end of the *Hurricane* as a day fighter in northwestern Europe. Thereafter it was relegated to ground support and anti-shipping duties, or to theatres further afield such as Malta, North Africa, and the Far East.

	Mark I	Mark II
Engine	Rolls Royce *Merlin* II or III of 1030 hp	Rolls Royce *Merlin* 24 or 27 of 1280 hp
Wingspan	40 feet 0 inches	40 feet 0 inches
Length	31 feet 5 inches	32 feet 0 inches
Empty Weight	4670 pounds	5150 pounds (Mk.IIa); 5640 pds (Mk.IIb); 5800 pds (Mk.IIc)
Loaded Weight	6600 pounds	8050 pounds (Mk.IIa); 8250 pds (Mk.IIb); 8100 pds (Mk.IIc)
Maximum Speed	318 mph (Watts prop) 324 mph (Rotol prop)	342 mph (Mk.IIa); 340 mph (Mk.IIb); 336 mph (Mk.IIc)
Service Ceiling	33,400 feet (Watts prop) 34,200 feet (Rotol prop)	36,300 feet (Mk.IIa); 36,000 feet (Mk.IIb); 35,600 feet (Mk.IIc)
Range on Internal Tanks	440 miles (Watts prop) 425 miles (Rotol prop)	470 miles (Mks. IIa and IIb) 460 miles (Mk.IIc)
Fixed Armament	eight .303 machine guns	Mk.IIa—as Mk.I; Mk.IIb—twelve .303 machine guns; Mk.IIc—four 20-mm cannon

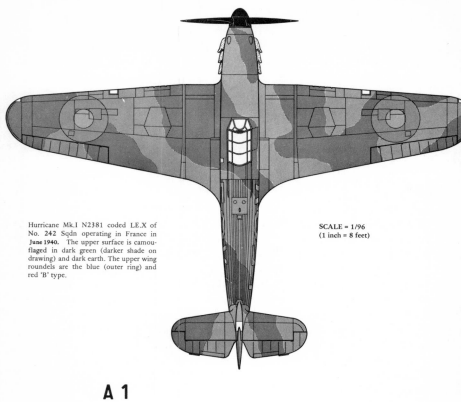

Hurricane Mk.I N2381 coded LE.X of No. 242 Sqdn operating in France in **June 1940.** The upper surface is camouflaged in dark green (darker shade on drawing) and dark earth. The upper wing roundels are the blue (outer ring) and red 'B' type.

SCALE = 1/96
(1 inch = 8 feet)

A 1

A 2

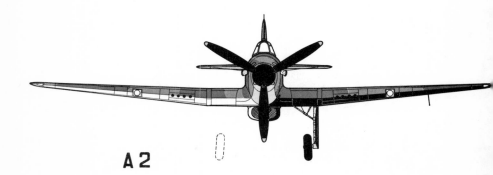

Front view of Hurricane N2381 showing the three-bladed Rotol propeller. The underside of the fuselage was doped aluminum, and the undersides of the wings, including the fuselage centre section and the radiator, were black (port) and white (starboard).

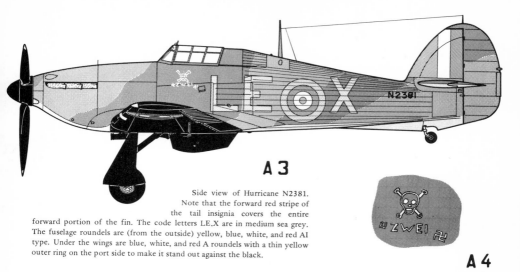

A 3

Side view of Hurricane N2381.
Note that the forward red stripe of
the tail insignia covers the entire
forward portion of the fin. The code letters LE.X are in medium sea grey.
The fuselage roundels are (from the outside) yellow, blue, white, and red AI
type. Under the wings are blue, white, and red A roundels with a thin yellow
outer ring on the port side to make it stand out against the black.

A 4

Personal marking in white under the port cockpit of N2381 LE.X. The two
swastikas and the German word for two, "ZWEI", presumably indicate two
victories. This aircraft had to be burned during the evacuation from France,
but it is interesting to speculate how the pilot intended to indicate future
victories.

SCALE = 1/72
(1 inch = 6 feet)

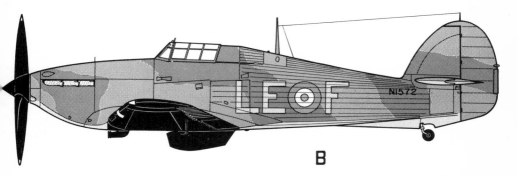

B

Hurricane Mk.I N1572 coded LE.F in early 1940. This aircraft is fitted with the two-bladed Watts propeller and, while it is in the same
colour scheme as N2381 LE.X, fin stripes, underwing roundels, and yellow outer rings to roundels have not yet been adopted.

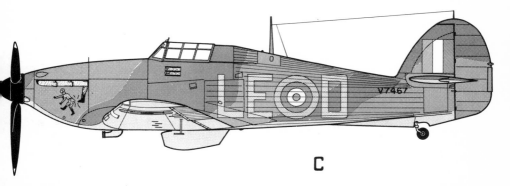

C

Hurricane Mk.I V7467 coded LE.D in September 1940. This aircraft is in the colour scheme used during the Battle of Britain with Sky
"S" undersurfaces and A type underwing roundels. This was the personal aircraft of S/L D.R.S. Bader, as indicated by the Squadron
Leader's pennant under the port side beneath the cockpit. It also carries the squadron motif on the port side of the nose (see C2).

C 2

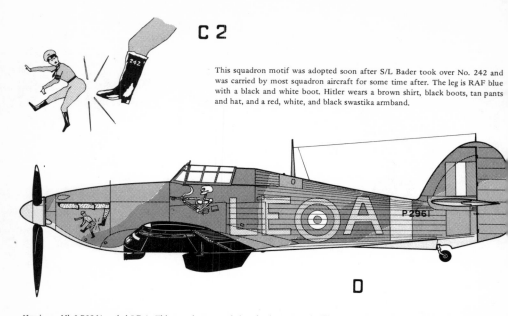

This squadron motif was adopted soon after S/L Bader took over No. 242 and was carried by most squadron aircraft for some time after. The leg is RAF blue with a black and white boot. Hitler wears a brown shirt, black boots, tan pants and hat, and a red, white, and black swastika armband.

D

Hurricane Mk.I P2961 coded LE.A. This was the personal aircraft of F/O W.L. "Willie" McKnight, who was probably the outstanding Canadian fighter pilot during the first two years of World War 2. It is seen as it appeared just before McKnight's death in action on 12 January 1941 and carries the scheme adopted by RAF Fighter Command immediately after the Battle of Britain. This included "S" undersurface except for black port wing fuselage centre section half, Sky spinner, and Sky rear fuselage band. Code letters remain medium sea grey.

D 2

McKnight's personal insignia was in white with a black outline.

D 3

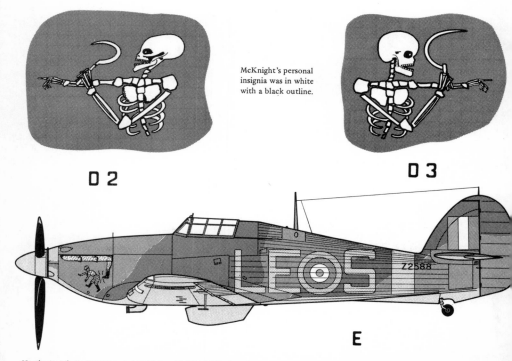

E

Hurricane Mk.IIa Z2588 coded LE.S in mid-1941. This aircraft has the portion of the nose immediately behind the spinner in worn Sky paint and all-Sky undersurfaces.

Bibliography

Allen, Hubert R., *Who Won the Battle of Britain?*, London, Barker, 1974.

Barton, A.E.M., *242 Squadron History and Notes*, Marham, n.p., 1963.

Beckles, Gordon, *Canada Comes to England*, London, Hodder and Stoughton, 1941.

Bowyer, Michael J.F., *2 Group R.A.F.: A Complete History, 1936-1945*, London, Faber, 1974.

Bowyer, Michael J.F., *The Stirling Bomber*, London, Faber, 1980.

Brickhill, Paul, *Reach for the Sky: The Story of Douglas Bader*, London, Collins, 1954.

Brittain, Sir Harry, *Come the Three Corners: Achievements of the Empire Overseas Since War Began*, London, Hutchinson, 1940.

Collier, Richard, *The Sands of Dunkirk*, London, Collins, 1961.

Deighton, Len, *Fighter: The True Story of the Battle of Britain*, London, J. Cape, 1977.

Douglas, Sholto, *Years of Command*, London, Collins, 1966.

Dowding, Sir Hugh, "The Battle of Britain", Supplement to *London Gazette*, 11 September 1946.

Dupérier, Bernard, *La Vieille Equipe*, Paris, Editions Berger-Levrault, 1946.

Ellis, L.F., *The War in France and Flanders, 1939-1940*, London, HMSO, 1953.

Field, Peter J., *Canada's Wings*, London, John Lane, 1942.

Gobeil, F.M., "We Patrol Dunkirk", *R.M.C. Review*, Kingston, June 1941.

Halley, James J., *Royal Air Force Aircraft L1000 to L9999*, Tonbridge, Air Britain, 1979.

Halley, James J., *Royal Air Force Aircraft N1000 to N9999*, Tonbridge, Air Britain, 1977.

Halley, James J., *Royal Air Force Aircraft P1000 to P9999*, Tonbridge, Air Britain, 1978.

Halliday, H.A., *The Tumbling Sky*, Stittsville, Canada's Wings, 1978.

Hitchins, F.H., *The All-Canadian Squadron*, n.p., ca 1942.

Hocking, Charles, *Dictionary of Disasters at Sea During the Age of Steam, 1824-1962*, London, Lloyd's Register, 1969.

Horne, Alistair, *To Lose a Battle: France 1940*, London, Macmillan, 1969.

Jones, Ira, *Tiger Squadron: The Story of No. 74 Squadron, R.A.F., in Two World Wars*, London, W.H. Allen, 1954.

Mason, Francis K., *Battle Over Britain*, London, McWhirter Twins, 1969.

Mason, Francis K., *Hawker Aircraft Since 1920*, (2nd edition), London, Putnam, 1971.

Price, Alfred, *Battle of Britain: The Hardest Day: 18 August 1940*, London, Macdonald and Jane's, 1979.

Ramsey, Sir Bertram, "The Evacuation of the Allied Armies From Dunkirk and Neighbouring Beaches", Supplement to *London Gazette*, 17 July 1947.

Ramsey, Winston G. (ed.), *The Battle of Britain Then and Now*, London, After the Battle Magazine, 1980.

Rawlings, John D.R., *Fighter Squadrons of the R.A.F. and Their Aircraft*, (2nd ed.), London, Macdonald and Jane's, 1978.

Shirer, William L., *The Collapse of the Third Republic*, London, William Heinneman, 1970.

Shores, Chris, *Aces High*, London, Neville Spearman, 1966.

Stacey, C.P., *Six Years of War*, Ottawa, Queen's Printer, 1955.

Turner, Stan P., "Over France", *The Canadians at War 1939-45*, Volume 1, Montreal, Reader's Digest, 1965.

170

Turner, Stan P., "No Horsing", *Airforce*, Volume 4, No. 3 (September 1980).

Wood, Derek (with Derek Dempster), *The Narrow Margin*, London, Hutchinson, 1961.

Wykeham, Peter, *Fighter Command: A Study of Air Defence, 1914-1960*, London, Putnam, 1960.

No. 242 Squadron

$\mathcal{I}ndex$

INDIVIDUALS

173

LOCATIONS

175

Frejus, France, 141
Frevent, France, 47
Furnes, France, 52, 58

G

Genoa, Italy, 141
Ghent, Belgium, 36
Gibraltar, 139
Glasgow, Scotland, 123
Goodwin Sands, England, 61
Grange Farm, England, 120
Gravesend, England, 103, 111
Guelph, Ontario, 14, 16
Guines, France, 116

H

Halifax, Nova Scotia, 16
Halton, England, 19
Hamilton, Ontario, 84
Hatfield, England, 36
Hawkinge, England, 51, 56
Hazebrouck, France, 130
Hendon, England, 30
Herne Bay, England, 111
High River, Alberta, 15
Hornchurch, England, 96, 101
Horsham, England, 129
Hucknall, England, 26

I

Invermay, Saskatchewan, 15
Isle of Wight, 16
Ipswitch, England, 122

J

Jansen, Saskatchewan, 15
Jersey, Channel Islands, 77

K

Kelowna, British Columbia, 23
Kenley, England, 35, 36, 104
Kincardine, Ontario, 15
Kingston, Ontario, 13
Kirkfield, Ontario, 15

L

Lancing, Ontario, 41
Le Cateau, France, 36, 39
Le Havre, France, 69, 70n
Le Mans, France, 67, 68, 73, 74, 77
Le Touquet, France, 37, 115, 134
Lille, France, 34, 36, 37, 39, 40, 43, 50,
    130, 131
Lille-Seclin, France, 30, 37
Liverpool, England, 19
London, England, 16, 23, 27, 42, 25, 83,
    89, 97, 100-102, 106, 108, 125, 136
London, Ontario, 15, 78
Louvain, Belgium, 34, 36
Luton, England, 112

M

Maidstone, England, 104
Maison Blanche, Algeria, 140

Malta, 139, 140
Manchester, England, 26
Manston, England, 33, 35n, 36, 40, 48,
    50-53, 55, 56, 58, 127, 131, 133-135
Marham, England, 141
Marigny, France, 69
Martlesham Heath, England, 112, 113,
    118, 122, 125
Menin, Belgium, 51
Merville, France, 39, 41, 127
Middlekirk, Belgium, 54, 126, 127
Minehead, England, 77, 78
Montreal, Quebec, 84, 124
Moorselle, Belgium, 34, 35n, 36

N

Nanaimo, British Columbia, 41
Nantes, France, 71, 73-75, 76n, 77
Nieuport, Belgium, 57, 59
Norrent Fontes, England, 35, 36
Northolt, England, 96
North Weald, England, 93, 94, 96, 98,
    101, 102, 119, 125, 131
Norwich, England, 88, 90, 112

O

Ostend, Belgium, 53, 54, 126, 127, 132,
    134
Ottawa, Ontario, 13, 16, 27, 113

P

Paris, France, 46, 71, 73, 74
Pas de Calais, France, 131
Passaic, New Jersey, 113
Ponders' End, England, 95
Port Hood, Nova Scotia, 41

R

Rennes, France, 71, 74, 75
Reims, France, 69
Rochford, England, 111
Rosetown, Saskatchewan, 15
Rossland, British Columbia, 113
Rye, England, 105

S

St. Athan, South Wales, 25
St. Inglevert, France, 116
St. Nazaire, France, 71, 72, 75, 76
St. Omer, France, 49, 127, 129, 130
St. Pol, France, 36
St. Thomas, Ontario, 64, 78
Saint John, New Brunswick, 92
Saskatoon, Saskatchewan, 14, 17, 92
Saumar, France, 71
Scapa Flow, Orkney Islands, 24, 25
Smith Falls, Ontario, 14
Souge, France, 71
Souris, Manitoba, 15
Southport, Florida, 113
Stratford, Ontario, 55
Stapleford Tawney, England, 125
Stoney Cross, England, 141
Summerland, British Columbia, 113

FORMATIONS

No. 242 Squadron